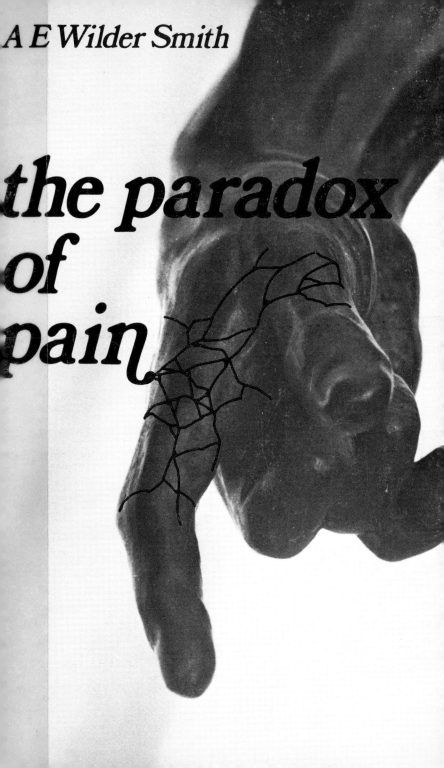

A E Wilder Smith

the paradox
of
pain

the paradox of pain

A E Wilder Smith

Harold Shaw Publishers
Wheaton, Illinois

The tortures occur. If they are unnecessary, then there is no God or a bad one. If there is a good God, then these tortures are necessary.

C. S. LEWIS

acknowledgements

This text has been prepared from a short presentation of the same subject which appeared several years ago under the title Warum lässt Gott es Zu? *That book was intentionally brief so that it could be placed in letters addressed to countries behind the Iron Curtain, where it has circulated widely for several years. The present work has been extended considerably and revised to meet the needs of English-speaking people in the Western world.*

As will appear from some parts of the text, the work of extension and revision was undertaken during the author's stay in Turkey as a visiting professor. Dr. Julian Richardson, Assistant Professor of Electrical Engineering, Middle East Technical University, Ankara, has made a number of helpful and constructive criticisms.

Finally, my wife has helped in many ways with the preparation of the text and its contents. Without her patience while living in Turkey in temporary quarters, the book would never have emerged.

foreword

This book is an attempt to search for meaning in the abyss of suffering, wrong, evil, blood, sweat, tears and anguish in which the human race finds itself. In a day when meaning is interpreted in terms of meaninglessness, any text involving more than a superficial interpretation of suffering is extremely difficult to write, to say nothing of interpreting the general subject matter.

However, in spite of the meaninglessness of life as taught from Darwin to Camus and in modern atheistic theology, the author believes that, in the long run, man's nature is rational, and that he will not rest until he has asserted himself as a rational being—even in the rationale of suffering. For, in spite of the admitted chaos surrounding us, tempting us to likewise disintegrate into chaos, every time a girl falls in love with a boy, they both find they begin to have meaning for one another whether they like it or not. Love is the great producer of meaning, even in suffering. Therefore, this text is aimed at those who have found or are finding some meaning or rationale in their life and would like to extend it to cover the problem of suffering. After all, we are all supplied with a large and complex organ known as the brain which is superb at untying knots of logic and meaning and is unhappy if it has no work to do. Presumably it was supplied us as a standard part that is to be used.

1

Thought and Action: Today and Yesterday

Few realize how differently people today use the process of thinking as compared to individuals of a hundred years ago. We live in an age of unprecedented technology and, therefore, of technological thought, so of necessity technological subject matter must color today's thought processes more than in the past. But this coloring of thought is not the essential factor. The generation gap has not resulted from a mere change of shades in thought, but by the adoption of entirely new thought modes or processes. Radical changes in the very mechanism of thought have occurred.

A century ago the average thinking person considered life and the universe to be orderly and to contain meaning. He willingly admitted that it was often difficult to discover the meaning and order behind things. But this fact did not disturb him in his basis of thought, namely, that order and meaning were there if he could only find them. Though human stupidity or weakness might distort and slow down the unraveling of meaning, the meaning was still there. The book of the universe and of life was hard to decode or read. But the average thinker was still convinced that it was a *code* capable of being deciphered if sufficient insight and intelligence could be brought to bear on it.

Based on such premises, huge efforts were easily justified in the effort to decipher the mysteries of the meaning and mechanisms of life and the universe. The overrun from this conviction can be seen today in the momentum still present in such efforts as molecular biology and space exploration, where laws, interpretation and meaning are being sought. However, it is not generally recognized that large areas of today's philosophy, art, music, general culture and even theology have abandoned the very premises which launched the huge scientific effort which has utterly changed the whole world of technology and science. Most practicing research scientists still work on the premise that nature is a code, and that life is a meaningful system governed by law and yielding its meaning to those who try hard and intelligently enough. But other branches of knowledge such as those mentioned above have more or less arrived at the conclusion that life and the universe are, in the last analysis, absurd and devoid of meaning. Camus is an example of this, for he received the Nobel Prize for saying just this in his own elegant way.

Thus, where our forefathers based their thought processes on the premise that life and the universe were meaningful, the generation gap in thought processes today is largely caused by exactly the opposite premise. Sartre, Camus and other modern thinkers have obtained the highest praise from today's intelligentsia for elegantly and cleverly purveying the premise that life, man and the universe are meaningless. It naturally follows, therefore, that suffering is meaningless too.

Only in such a cultural atmosphere were scientific theories such as those of Darwin able to take root and flourish both in scientific and popular circles. For Darwin, aided by Huxley, propagated the view—using mountains of scientific detail as evidence—that all life processes arose *spontaneously—without motivation or rationale*—from randomness. In the last analysis, randomness is congruent with lack of order and, therefore, with lack of meaning. According to this view, the mixtures of amino acids which are supposed to have given spontaneous birth to life showed no *meaning* or *motivation* behind them. No volition guided them and other building blocks into the codes of meaning which make up DNA as we know it today. The first proteins and nucleic acids allegedly arose spontaneously from meaninglessness. This boils down to saying that if there is any meaning in life or its origin at all, that meaning must be based, in the last analysis, on sheer meaninglessness. The same applies to life's destiny—it must be meaningless too. And, if meaning is founded and grounded on meaninglessness, how else can meaning be defined except as meaninglessness!

EQUATING FACT TO NONFACT

Thus, biological sciences are also mixed up in the change in thought processes which have so radically altered the modern world. Consider the lengths to which scientific philosophers such as Sir Julian Huxley have gone. He teaches all who will listen that human and social order flourish better if humans believe in a god or support a religion of some sort, for their belief helps them respect each other. Therefore, he advocates the propagation of some sort of belief in a god external to nature, even though he says that we, the enlightened ones, well know that such a belief does not correspond to the actual facts of nature, but is thoroughly false and deceptive. "Religion today is imprisoned in a theistic frame of ideas," he claims, "compelled to operate in the unrealities of the dualistic world. In the unitary humanistic frame it acquires a new look and new freedoms. With the aid of our new vision it has the opportunity of escaping from the theistic impasse and of playing its proper role in the real world of unitary existence."[1]

Schaeffer rightly observes: "Now it may be true that it can

be shown by observation that society copes better with life through believing that there is a god. But, in that case, surely optimistic humanism is being essentially unreasonable . . . if, in order to be optimistic, it rests upon the necessity of mankind believing and functioning upon a lie."

In other words, human society demonstrably needs to believe in a god to function properly and optimally. "All right," says today's scientific philosopher, "let them carry on with that belief if it helps them function, even though, strictly speaking, it is a lie." Huxley has no objection to believing in "anti-facts" (believing in a non-existent god) if that allows man to go on being optimistically humanist.

Consider the chaos implicit in this kind of thought pattern. Huxley is a scientific humanist who believes in "unitary existence"—no divine existence outside human existence. This means that there is no thought (Descartes' proof of existence) besides human (or possibly animal) thought. Yet, the human thought he uses is calmly allowed to be no-thought, for there is no objection to holding a nongod to be a real god!

Surely everyone, including the rationalist, believes that man is a rational being and that rationality is a part—an integral part—of every man. To postulate that man, in order to function, must be nonrational is surely to destroy an integral part of man, his rationality. This must divide and destroy his very being, because this is believing a nonfact to be a fact just for the sake of its usefulness. This is the position to which scientific philosophy in some quarters—and they are influential quarters—has led us. This line must destroy the very nature of thought and rationality and, therefore, rational man himself. Not only is this the main line in present-day intellectual thought. The general public also thinks this way. Not only do gifted intellectuals like Huxley, Camus and Sartre propagate these views, but Fellini and Antonioni of Italy, Slessinger of England and Bergman of Sweden are all actively proclaiming the same "irrational rationalism" in their films. Thus, the view that life is meaningless is not merely the property of the high-brows but is being claimed by so-called lowbrows too. Popular mass education is seeing to this. Nobel prizes are doled out to those who are responsible for teachings that are destroying man, the rational one!

Former generations used as their thought basis the premise that, if a fact is demonstrably true, then it was a suitable starting point for further thought, belief and action. Thought processes were rather absolute in their methodology. Today such "naïveté" is no longer permissible. In current thought, a nonfact is allowable, without any difficulty, as a basis for belief—if it is useful (e.g., Huxley's allowance of the divinity concept). Thus the sharply different functions of facts and nonfacts have been blurred in modern philosophical thought and one will serve for the other as importunity demands. The fact (truth) is equated with the nonfact (untruth).

HOW FAITH IS ARRIVED AT

But how can one get a man to believe in a nonfact in the same way that our fathers believed in demonstrable facts? That is the grand feat which modern thought has now accomplished with Kirkegaard's aid. A new methodology was developed especially for this one purpose—how to believe in and be convinced of nonfacts and make them the basis of our faith.

The pattern is quite simple. If a man can see no rational sense, rhyme nor reason in life and its problems, if he cannot find any way of decoding life's mysteries, then he must no longer seek the solutions by rational thought. He must close his eyes, throw life's textbook into the corner, and take a "leap of faith" based on nonfact. Thus nonfacts (blind leaps) are now serving the purpose formerly monopolized by facts as a foundation for thought and faith. Theology professors have faith in faith rather than faith in a fact or a person.

It is vitally important to realize how different this method of thought is as compared to that employed by the prophets throughout Holy Scripture. In the Acts of the Apostles Paul the apostle is reported to have *reasoned* with the elders with tears day and night about matters of *faith*.[2] He was ready to throw his faith overboard if it did not comply with the known facts. If the body of the Lord Jesus Christ could have been found after his death and resurrection, that one fact would have abolished at one stroke all Christian faith and doctrine forever. For the whole Christian position (faith) turned (and turns) on this one outstanding *fact*—the Lord rose from the dead as he had promised before his death. His body was transmuted from material mortality to the supramortal, to immortality. The disproving of this *one central fact*—the pillar of faith which was attested to by more than five hundred living people at the time Paul wrote of the resurrection—would have destroyed Christianity.

In those days Christians did not arrive at their faith by a leap of faith in the dark, but by basing their thought processes —and therefore their faith—on the fact of Christ's resurrection. Any other way of arriving at real Christian faith stands forever outside the testimony of Scripture as well as that of living Christians. The methodology then, as now, remains the same if we wish to arrive at the same assurance of faith: having assessed the evidence for the facts, we base on them our thought, and therefore our action and faith.

CAUSES OF THE MODERN GENERATION GAP

Much of the gap between the generations today is due to each generation—the older and the younger—not recognizing differences in the other's basic methods of thought. Thinkers of today, such as Camus, Sartre and Huxley, are perfectly willing to base their beliefs and actions on nonfacts, simply because they believe the world is absurd and devoid of rationale and meaning. As a result, nonfacts are replacing facts in our thought and belief processes. If the facts of history are no longer needed as the foundation for our faith and thought, on what then shall we build? On nonfacts, of course! Today it is believed that there is a logical and intellectual *chasm* between faith and nonfaith and that the intellectual way across is as pathless as an abyss. In fact, it is maintained that only a blind leap will transport us across the chasm. *Both the new theology as well as scientific rationalism use this leap over the chasm.* Huxley arrives at his optimistic faith in humanism by allowing his nonfactual god-belief, his believing in something or someone he knows not to be there, to be in fact there! Perhaps it is here that the reason lies for older generations not understanding the younger!

THE EXASPERATED STUDENT

I once knew a student who disliked higher mathematics, yet needed this knowledge to pass his examinations. After many futile attempts to master a chapter of a rather abstruse aspect of the subject, he threw the book into the corner of his room, muttering that it was all bunk and nonsense—*to him*. But it was not nonsense to everyone. For others had mastered the same contents and extracted meaning from them. The difficulty was that the student, being unable to comprehend the message of the abstruse chapter, concluded that it was absurd nonsense. *His conclusion was, unfortunately for him, wrong.*

Camus and others are saying, in effect, the same thing—life is absurd and meaningless—*to them*. But other serious people, although usually the first to admit that life's book is hard to decipher, confess to having found satisfying solutions to at least some of life's problems. And their conclusions are based on the facts given by events of history such as the resurrection of Christ. And more and more problems and seeming paradoxes may be resolved into order by the careful and logical application of thought.

THE AGE OF REASON

Our much-prized age of reason has regressed into an age of

nonreason. The age of scientific philosophy has reverted to an age of non- or anti-philosophy. What else can we conclude if leaders of modern thought say that they're willing to believe in the existence of a god who they really don't think exists, in order to hold onto their optimistic humanism? Learning and philosophy are dependent upon the communication of *meaning and message.* Is it any wonder that communication between man and man, generation and generation, is breaking down because the message of the communication allegedly has been found to be meaningless? In this way philosophy today has become, in fact, an antiphilosophy, just as the age of reason has become an age of unreasonable blind leaps of faith in a pitch-black unreasonable and absurd world—of the kind described by Camus.

The whole situation as seen by our present world philosophy can be well summed up in these lines by Hans Arp, one of the original members of the Dada group:

> The head downward
> the legs upward
> he tumbles into the bottomless
> from whence he came
>
> like a dish covered with hair
> like a four-legged sucking chair
> like a deaf echo trunk
> half full half empty
>
> the head downward
> the legs upward
> he tumbles into the bottomless
> from whence he came

Francis Schaeffer comments: "On the basis of modern man's methodology, whether expressed in philosophy, art, literature or theology, there can be no other ending than this—man tumbling into the bottomless."

PICASSO IN CHICAGO

Two years ago I was standing in front of the Civic Center in Chicago where stands a huge abstract sculpture by Picasso, for which the mayor of Chicago paid a large sum of money. While I was determining from which angles it would be best to photograph this piece of art, a well-mannered Chicagoan quietly asked why I was going to all the trouble. I said I wanted to get the effect and meaning in real life faithfully reproduced on film. His answer was quite interesting. He said that since in his opinion the work carried and expressed no communicable meaning in real life, it was a waste of time and good film to try to reproduce it in a photo!

ATHEISTIC CLERGYMEN

Picasso again demonstrates the tendency of modern art to detach itself from the realities and facts of life and, in doing so, to lose meaning for many people. Theology, the proverbial laggard in modern intellectual activity, has followed philosophy, art and music, albeit at a distance of some years. I spoke to a young German clergyman recently just before he was to conduct a confirmation service. In all earnestness he informed me that he, as a pastor, believed that there was no God behind the universe, although he would not yet dare to say so openly in his church. He believed in an atheistic theology. Theology being the science of the study of divinity or God, we have arrived at the position of a pastor studying the science of no-God, which we may equate to nothingness, for a god that does not exist is nothing. So the conclusion was that he had spent seven years studying nothingness! I pointed out this rather elementary fact to him. He retreated in some confusion, saying that I had misunderstood him. He did not say, he explained that he believed in an *atheistic* theology, but rather, in an *a-theistic* theology. This was *quite* different, he said, for it meant that he could continue in his theology *without* God— that is, a-theistically rather than *atheistically*! One wonders what sort of a shepherd of his flock such a young man will make when he has to comfort the dying and lay hands on the sick and those wracked with pain.

CONSEQUENCES

But why bother to go into all this theory and philosophy? If there is no meaning behind the universe and life, why try to find any? Why thresh so much straw when there is such a lot of wheat about?

The reason is simple. Man is a rational being and cannot, therefore, be happy without exercising his rationality. To ask the rational being to live in and for meaninglessness or non-rationality is to ask the rational being to destroy himself. He goes into despair, for which, apparently, he was not designed. For he will not rest, if he is honest with himself, until he leaves the despair by replacing meaninglessness with meaning and order. This applies to the meaning of suffering too.

If contemporary rational thinkers—being rational beings—see injustice, war, suffering, violence and apparent meaninglessness on every side, they cannot *rest* until they have found a rationale of some sort for it all. Huxley admits that he is prepared to be an optimistic humanist on the basis of believing in a nonexistent god—one he knows not to be there, but whose presence and existence we must postulate to keep ourselves happy. But the use of a nonrationality, a lie, a nonfact, to keep a man "rational" and happy, will surely destroy the very basis of rationality!

No, if rational man is to remain rational and not destroy the integral part of himself called rationality, he must use fact "like it is" to find some meaning for all the apparent chaos and meaninglessness which surround him. How can he rationally explain a beautiful young mother dying of cancer while her child is being born? How can he avoid despair on seeing men, women and children mutilated by war, hunger and pestilence? These are realities. Camus shrugged his shoulders at such sights, sensitive as he was, and saw things exceedingly clearly, and said that the world and life are meaningless jokes —absurd. They represent no code, they carry no meaning.

Jesus Christ saw similar suffering and spoke of the beggar Lazarus covered with sores and lying at the rich man's gate. He had mercy and compassion on the beggar. But he did not leave it at that and shrug it all off, just as if life and Lazarus were meaningless victims of a harsh, absurd and cruel world. He interpreted Lazarus' apparently meaningless suffering—and the rich man's riches too—and told us in no uncertain terms in Luke 16:20-25 what they *meant.*

But today's teachers of Christianity have not given convincing answers to the modern "meaningless" theorists, even though Christ's interpretation of the problem is on hand if they care to read and believe it. The fact is, of course, that Christ's interpretation of Lazarus' suffering, and of other problems involving suffering, is not generally accepted today. The real reason for the unwillingness to accept his interpretation is coupled to an unwillingness to accept the full fact and impact of resurrection as evidenced in Christ's own body. If we really believed in Christ's and our own resurrection as unshakable facts, we wouldn't have the slightest difficulty in accepting Christ's interpretation of the "mystery" or apparent "meaninglessness" of Lazarus' suffering. We have become so used to equating nonfact with fact that we find it difficult to rigidly follow the logical consequences of believing in a real fact! For, in Lazarus' case the introduction of one overlooked fact, namely, personal resurrection, reduced the hopelessness and meaninglessness of his sufferings to meaningfulness. Of course, if the "fact" of resurrection is, in reality, one of our famous "nonfacts," then we must shrug our shoulders on seeing Lazarus and mutter with Camus, "Absurd!"

Christ, however, kept steadily before him as he explained Lazarus' case the fact of personal resurrection, which he was shortly to experience in his own body. To the humanist bystander, tied up in Huxley's ideas about "unitary existence," Lazarus as he lay there full of sores was a senseless cruelty, an example of callous torture of innocent humanity. But if the promise of recompense and correction—in fact, the mighty recompense of resurrection—is a fact, then, of course, meaninglessness resolves itself to meaning. For surely if a short term of suffering is the method by which eternal nonsuffering or bliss is to be obtained, then Lazarus was in for a bargain—to put it mildly—and reasonableness is restored to apparent unreasonableness.

The important thing is that by inserting an overlooked fact into our sequence of thought, chaos is often reduced to order, and meaninglessness to meaning. What modern philosophers have been busy doing—indeed, philosophers of all time have practiced the same art—is removing by unbelief certain facts from the sad case of this suffering world, facts given us by God himself to enable us to handle the problem intellectually. *Just as the addition of an overlooked fact (resurrection) brought meaning into the meaningless in the case of Lazarus' suffering, so the removal of some fact will reduce it from meaning and rationality to meaninglessness and irrationality.* We interpret and diagnose on the basis of all the facts of a case, that is, *we appoint meaning in the light of all relevant facts. But, remove the facts, even the revealed facts of the Bible, and meaninglessness and inability to diagnose the case must result because the resulting picture is incomplete.*

MAN CANNOT LIVE WITHOUT RATIONALITY

I have risked writing this book—an attempt to find meaning in a world of chaos and pain—for one main reason. It is obviously useless to argue reasonably with anyone who does not believe in meaning and, therefore, in reason. Many modern theologians and philosophers are in just this position. But this is not the case with a majority of the younger generation. For they are increasingly discovering that they cannot live with the doctrines popular in their own generation. Therefore they are seeking something better, something more in line with their experience. This is one of the reasons for the almost universal rebellion against the "establishment," the "establishment" which preaches meaninglessness today as well as that of the "status quo" of a century ago.

One reason for this rebellion against and dissatisfaction with the universal atmosphere of meaninglessness is quite unexpected. Young people, perhaps firm believers in Camus and Sartre, are finding that they cannot help falling in love with one another, just as their forefathers did. Girls are still pretty and boys are still attracted to their beauty of body and psyche. They become aware of the remarkable fact that falling in love with each other, in spite of what they have learned about the absurdity of everything, is not so absurd. In fact, it is giving their lives a totally new meaning whether they like it or not! Love is a new, hitherto neglected, fact and it transforms their lives, giving them purpose where they had imagined there was no purpose. The addition of one fact—human love is a fact, not a nonfact—to their lives has resolved some of life's meaninglessness to meaning.

The fact of love had been overlooked, but it now must be taken into account in the formula for life, just as in the case of the fact of resurrection which altered the equation dealing with Lazarus' suffering. The fact of love brings new rationality and new meaning, just as other facts—beauty in nature, order in the biological cell, chemical laws in biochemistry, and electromagnetic laws in valency help us see order where previously, without knowledge of these facts, meaninglessness reigned.

Because so many of the younger generation are finding their way back to rationality against the strong current of propaganda for the doctrine of absurdity (as evidenced by the giving of Nobel Prizes to its propagators), I have written this attempted apologetic on the problem of suffering, which bothers so many thinkers as being irrational and therefore meaningless. To do this I have tried *to add overlooked facts to the formula.* It is my sincere hope that the views on suffering presented here do not turn out to be glib or facile. Anyone born during the First World War and who has spent his young manhood in the Second World War has certainly been confronted with the anguish of the problem of pain, injustice and death in the prime of life. He has had the advantage of all this experience, in addition to having experienced the woes to which each man is heir, regardless of the period in which he was born. The author does not claim to be any exception. He hopes that the trials and dreadful sights to which he and his generation have been exposed have turned up new facts and experiences which, when added to the equation of suffering, will help to reduce it a little more to meaningfulness.

The following, then, is an attempt to enable us to regard the problem of suffering and evil without losing our nature as rational beings. For to lose our rationality is to lose our humanity, or, as Schaeffer would say, our "mannishness."

There are, of course, gaps in any arguments of the type presented here. There may be holes in the logic. The author thinks he sees some of them. But the whole work is an attempt to show that the doctrines of despair, which are the fashion today, are intellectually untenable and that they inevitably destroy man as a rational being, reducing him to the level of the brute. They arise by our neglecting certain facts of the problem. If we persist in them they will totally destroy our humanity. If the opposite doctrines, which are set out here— albeit imperfectly—are pursued, they will integrate our humanity and make us, in the words of the Bible, "whole" both in mind as well as in body and spirit.

IS THERE A PLACE FOR "BLIND FAITH"?

Someone will be sure to object to this kind of presentation, saying that, after all, the heavy emphasis on reason and rationality excludes the exercise of real faith as the evidence of things not seen but hoped for.

This kind of objection would be valid if one believed that reason is faith. But we have not said that. We have said that *evidence and facts should lead to faith and that nonfacts should not.* To build faith on a sound basis we must have sound facts and not flabby nonfacts or meaninglessness. When the facts of a case have been established beyond doubt, for example, that Christ (in this case) did, as an historical fact, rise from the dead on the third day, then we can start building faith on that fact. For, by being resurrected after death, as he had promised before dying, he proved that he had knowledge which ordinary mortals do not possess about the after-death state. In fact, the predicted and fulfilled resurrection proves that he had divine foreknowledge, and his words bore the weight attributable to divinity. If his words on resurrection have thus been proved to be divine, then surely what he says about me, my death, and my resurrection by his power will be divine. These divine facts and words allow me sufficient basis on which to build my faith by trusting in and acting on them. *This kind of building on divine evidence and facts, this trusting of them and their author, is nothing less and nothing more than biblical faith.*

All that this really means is that we are objecting to "blind" faith—leaps in the dark. I am well aware that at times I have no facts or evidence to build upon—probably as Lazarus had no evidence as he lay in misery. I am completely at sea in regard to belief and faith in those difficult situations when I do not know where I am nor what I should do or think. And I am often in that anguished position.

But it is when I am in such deep waters that I take a new look at the *facts of divine illumination, help and guidance that I have previously experienced.* Looking back, I see how God has kept his good hand over me, even in allowing apparent catastrophes. Recalling past facts and evidence, I base my faith for the future and the present on *them* and so reestablish trust (or faith in him) for the present where I cannot yet see the needed evidence. But I cannot base *trust* on nothing, nothingness or meaninglessness. I cannot leap in the dark. I trusted *him* in the past; he helped. Is that not fact and evidence that the same will be true of the present and the future, even in ultimate catastrophe? These facts strengthen me to trust him, the great personal Fact, *now* where I see no evidence. Such faith is by no means *blind*. It is based on a hindsight experience of him, on facts and on reason. But it is not based on nothing or nonfacts and therefore unaccountableness. Even in the dark of tribulation and the unknown my wavering faith is held steady by being founded upon him and his accomplished work on the cross, plus my past personal experience of his keeping faith with me. This is the basis for a trust founded upon solid fact. On this basis we treat the problem of suffering.

chapter

2

The Pink Professor

When I was a student of natural sciences in England, some of our lectures were given by a professor who had marked leftist tendencies. His lectures at the university were the poorest we ever endured. He'd bring a load of scientific journals into the lecture hall, open them, apparently at random, and then, equally at random, just talk. But he was a gentleman and was kind, in his reserved way, to all of us.

A complete transformation took place in the evenings when he went into town and stood on a soapbox to harangue the masses with the verve and skill of the convinced revolutionary. He was nobly rewarded by his leftist political friends when they gained control of the country, for he soon became a peer, with the title of "lord," and was appointed an important administrator of a big university.

This professor was, in common with many Marxist theorists, a convinced and militant atheist. One day he came into the laboratory, unnoticed by me, as I was talking to another student about things other than purely materialistic science. I remarked that, not surprisingly, the study of matter would probably yield only information about matter. Transmaterial matters might exist, but they would be overlooked by such methods. One could not expect to pick up ultraviolet light with a film sensitive only to infrared light. But even if infrared paper showed nothing that would not prove that no ultraviolet wavelengths existed. I saw no reason not to believe in God merely because our instruments had not detected him. Perhaps they were not on the same wavelength.

Overhearing these remarks, our professor exploded. "It really is a mystery to me," he said, "how otherwise intelligent people can say they believe in any god, let alone in a good and wise one, whom they call a person. We can explain the whole universe and all of life without resorting to the outdated and unnecessary postulate of a god behind it all. Chance and long time spans will do all that your theologians imagine he did without ever appealing to such nonsense as the 'Old Man in the Skies.' "

He continued: "It really is beyond my comprehension that intelligent people today could be still taken in by the same old drivel. I can understand cannibals in the jungle talking as you do. But not a student of the natural sciences in the twentieth century. It is bad enough to have people believing theoretically in a god behind things. But you people are much worse. You believe you have a personal sort of friendship with this god of yours and think you will therefore get preferential treatment from him. I can understand, perhaps, some old people saying they believe in some sort of mysterious spirit when they see a sunrise, a beautiful face, a rose or an orchid. But it is proof positive of lack in intelligence on the part of those same people when they do not take the time to see the other side of the coin. They have not the courage to see the other side and boldly throw out their mythical gods—the cowards!"

Having switched into his soapbox mood, our professor was in dead earnest—and angry. "People must be lacking in IQ if they do not see the other side of the picture which wipes out all the sunset and beauty stuff." He continued by talking about the cat stalking the mouse and playing with it, letting it totter away half dead, and then grabbing it again at the last minute in its horrible claws. Then, when the poor mouse did not have the strength to provide any more fun for the cat, it squeezed the life out of its tattered body, biting its head off with a juicy crunch, and purring with delight at the evening's entertainment. "It is marvelous that your intelligent, almighty, all-loving and kind god prepared both the mouse in its helplessness and the cat with its talon strength and cruel mentality. That is a beautiful proof of the goodness of your god," he said, with a look of profound scorn in my direction.

I shrank into my corner of the laboratory, but he had not finished with me. "What about the young mother dying of cancer, her body stinking with decay before they take the baby from her and put her in her coffin? Is that your proof of the great Creator who made all things well—all things bright and beautiful? The Lord God made them all," he hissed. "And what about your capitalists who have worn down the working masses for centuries and built your churches to help you do it? We are going to alter all that—and quickly, believe me!

"What disgusts me," he said, "is the rank hypocrisy of it all." After a pause to regain his poise, he added, "What about all the agony—the agony of the father and children left behind when they bury the mother? What about the lifetimes of hunger suffered by the poor in India and Russia? Did your good god create all that as well as the sunrises and the laughing faces?" Looking grimly at me, he leaned across the table and said slowly, "Because, if he did—if he did make the disgusting, the cruel and the nauseating, as well as the beautiful—then I, for one, would believe him to be a devil and not a god. Only a devil could make the apparently beautiful and then mock us all with the anguish of the disgusting. But, as I am not so medieval as to believe either in devils, or gods, for that matter,

I regard the whole argument as a pure wanton waste of time, not worthy of mention in a scientific laboratory."

Having unburdened his soul, he regained some of his professorial aplomb and smilingly looked around for any answers that might be forthcoming. I mumbled something to the effect that his was only one side of the question. Other great people had no difficulty in maintaining an entirely opposite view.

"Let us leave out the question of wars and suffering caused by man himself," he said. "We might explain problems caused by man directly as due to his not being evolved far enough away from his animal ancestors. If we wait long enough, he will evolve higher and get better. Let us leave that and look at another field to which no one has ever honestly turned with a reply that was satisfactory to me. What about the refinement of torture we see all around us which has nothing whatever to do with man's nature? Take the designed torture we can all see in the transmission of the malarial parasite. It shows signs of what looks like careful, thoughtful planning with the single purpose of plaguing and torturing the host animal—or man. To me the whole system looks like a remarkable sort of planning, if a good god worked it all out. As I said before, if you want plan behind the universe and life, this sort of setup and planning seems to show a good and a bad, a kindly and a vindictive planner all in one—a god who is a devil."

Musing, he continued, "No, I just cannot believe this religious stuff myself. It really is just too ridiculous. My intelligence and my common sense force me to reject the whole bag of nonsense. I am near enough to being a nihilist, you tell me. But I should become an absolute nihilist if I were to force myself to believe in a god who is a devil. An almighty god, such as you believe in, and a good god, just could not show so many evidences of what appear to be thoughtful, planned goodnesses, such as sunrises and other beauties, and at the same time so many signs of cold, calculated, intelligent sadism. If you were able to develop sufficient logic," he said, scornfully addressing himself directly to me, "you would have recognized long ago that *your* views lead directly to nihilism. Can you imagine any supreme, almighty, personal being, who was at the same time all-wise and all-good and yet frightfully vindictive and bad, planning all sorts of plagues and diseases as well as the beauty of the rising sun and healthy body? It just does not make sense. It is plain bunk." He turned from me in contempt.

There was quiet for a short while. Then he began once more: "Of course, you people can always try to get around the difficulty by actually assuming a devil, who surprised the all-knowing and the all-powerful, almighty one by upsetting his applecart when he was not looking. I suppose you people attribute the disease, cancer, war, exploitation of the workers, and all the rest of this world's woes to a devil, do you not? But do you not realize that if god were almighty and good, wishing us—the so-called creatures of his hand—well, he must have neutralized the machinations of your devil before he got to work with his hosts of wicked angels in which you, no doubt, believe? Then the devil could not have been a source of devilry, could he? Of course, if your god is not almighty with respect to the devil, then there is only one thing to say about him: he is not god at all any more. So you destroy him this way if you do not destroy him the other way. If god cannot get even with the devil, then the devil must be a god too; and we are once more reduced to the primitive ideas of warring gods and devils in heaven and hell. You are not suggesting that we revert to ideas like that, are you? They held up intellectual progress and emancipation for centuries. I shall consider you an enemy of all true progress if you have the effrontery to inform me in a scientific laboratory that you believe in that sort of trash," he said, looking hard at me.

I am afraid most of us were rather like the proverbial rabbit when confronted by the snake—transfixed. No answers seemed to be able to formulate themselves in our brains. After all, our professor was a learned man. He was not just repeating slogans learned in Marxist circles. Obviously he was thoroughly convinced of his views. His extreme seriousness made him willing to stand up on a soapbox and confront the mob—an act which must have been rather humiliating for a professor of his standing. Although he was almost useless as a lecturer and professor in the classroom and experimental laboratory, we all respected him as a man, even though not all of us liked his convictions on political or religious matters.

While we were thinking about these things, he quietly started again. "I used to say," he continued, "that I was an agnostic and therefore could say nothing for certain about religious matters. But now that I am getting more mature and experienced, I have come to the conclusion that I am in reality a total atheist. I have been forced to the point where I do not believe in any god, either good or bad. That is, I believe neither in a good god nor in a bad devil. Such beliefs raise more difficulties than they remove. They just complicate matters. So, today, I just leave religious subjects outside my realm of thought—like alchemy. And I do not like people raising them in the classroom either. They only confuse, being highly unscientific and subjective. I do not need to blur my intellectual horizon with such primitive methods of thought any longer. The Marxists are not altogether wrong when they call religion 'opium for the people.' It is just that; it muddles their thoughts, blurs their vision and, because they then can see clearly no more, renders them an easy prey for the capitalists who are just waiting to exploit them for their own benefit."

THE SPOKESMAN OF MANY THINKING PEOPLE
I have never forgotten that afternoon in the laboratory. Certainly our professor had thought more about these matters than we students had. Moreover, he understood the problems of the ordinary thinking men and, when he wished, could be an excellent spokesman for them. Because he understood

them, he could sway them when he spoke. He never spoke with such conviction on cold, matter-of-fact chemical matters, but no one could get across ideas like he when revolution and Marxism came up.

The subject raised that afternoon in the laboratory is the very question occupying the minds of many thinking people. It looms large in the life of the person who, though satiated with life's material goods and apparently concerned only with pleasure and prosperity, is brought face to face with life's cruelties and suffering every day in his newspaper and on radio and television news, and is jolted by what is happening around him in his own life. If God is almighty—and if he is *God*, he must be almighty—why doesn't he stop all this chaos, all these wars, all the unrighteousnesses, injustice, misery and suffering in this world? Why did he ever let them start? Mere *men* everywhere are bending all their efforts to do what they can to stop it all. But, fortunately or unfortunately, men are not almighty and therefore cannot reach their goal.

Years ago a student friend crippled with polio told me, "If you want me to believe in your God, I shall expect him first of all to make a better job of the world we live in—and of me." I spent a good deal of time with him and he was apparently glad to listen to me. In my student enthusiasm I explained not only the Christian way of salvation by Christ's works, but also the intricacies of prophecy and the end of the age. Afterward he turned to me and said that now that he knew the way, he didn't need to do anything about it. For, when he saw the end coming, he would quickly accept God's way and be all right forever! A year or two later he was stricken with a stroke one Sunday morning while shaving. He died in seconds, without a sound. His wife found him an hour or so later.

If God loves us men and women, as the Bible assumes he does, why doesn't he end all misery and immediately set up a workable, orderly system such as most men of good will would like and for which they are striving? Doesn't he care for us any longer? If he doesn't care and has forgotten us, why should we care about him? Because he has allowed evil to exist along with good, thus apparently compromising himself in his omnipotence, many thinking people despair of an answer, or become atheists, just as my professor had done.

THE PROBLEM IS NOT NEW

Before further consideration of this question, we must remind ourselves that it is by no means new. Some have the mistaken idea that they are very modern if they handle the question as my professor did. They think that it stamps them as being advanced thinkers in having recognized that mankind is facing a new problem—and that they have solved it in a particularly new way.

Of course, this is not the case. When thistles and the thorns sprang up after mankind's first couple had fallen from the paradise of God by disobedience, they probably asked the same sort of question. Why indeed did God allow all this? Does he no longer love us and care for us? It looks as if he does not, for the very ground we cultivate does not bring forth its harvest any more. The birth of Cain was probably accompanied by pain, which was capped when he became his brother's murderer. How can *that* grisly history coincide with God's goodness and omnipotence?

Job could have asked the same kind of questions when the messengers came to him, one after another, each reporting a worse catastrophe to his family. It got so bad that Job cursed the day he had been born. He lost everything, including his health. Even his wife deserted him, telling him to curse God and die. How could Job believe in a holy, perfect, omnipotent God, concerned about him and his family, when all the catastrophes about him pointed in the opposite direction? He is God. He could have stopped it if he had wanted to. Did he want to find a way out for Job? and if not, was he a sadist? Did he still care about Job in allowing all this happen to the poor innocent man? The testimony of God and man was that Job was perfect—and innocent. Yet it all happened, and no explanation was forthcoming—until right at the end of the book of Job. If God did not care about poor, innocent, perfect Job, why should Job *love* God?

It is true of course, that there was still a great deal in Job and Adam's worlds which pointed to God's care in spite of thorns and thistles and catastrophes. But it is also true that there is just as much in our world. At the *beginning* of Adam's career the picture pointing to God's care and love was clear. In that earlier world everything indicated only God's care and omnipotence. But now Adam was outside paradise in a world of murderous and slain sons, thistles and thorns. Job had lost his family and fortune as well as the heart of his wife. The picture had become mixed and was full of chaos, full of circumstances which made it hard for the actors in those plays to believe in God's care and omnipotence. Many things now pointed away from this direction, and the area of God's order had retreated into quite a minute spot on the stage of life. So the same sort of contradictions arose in Adam and Job's times as they do now. Thus, the problem is by no means new. It is as old as mankind.

Accordingly, the question presents itself as follows: "Why should we be asked to believe and trust in a good God, thereby flying in the face of all—or at least a good deal of—the contemporary evidence?" One physicist put it as follows: "Why does God value *faith in him* so much as to make it the very condition, according to the Christian way of life, of entry into his kingdom? It seems most unfair to me. For faith means believing right in the face of contradictory evidence. Faith, to me, is merely the result of forcing myself to believe and trust in God's goodness and care when a goodly part of the evidence on hand leads me to reject such trust. Most preachers seem to preach faith as though it were the faculty of believing something which is not true—forcing oneself to believe and act in spite of evidence to the contrary. Why should God value a faith which acts against all common sense and evidence? Such action short circuits one of our highest faculties: the ability to weigh evidence and then act on it. Faith believes what is cannot see; it accepts evidence it cannot weigh. Why should God make as a condition of entering his presence and kingdom our ability to short circuit, abuse, and render null and void the very logic and evidence-weighing faculty with which the Bible says he endowed us? God gave us logical ability. Why does he demand that we act and think illogically in faith as a condition of entering his kingdom?"

To return to our first line of approach to this problem, then the question is: If the same Being planned both the good and the bad, the beautiful and the ugly, the sadistic and the loving, then all serious, logical, reasoning thought about him becomes impossible with our thinking faculties.

ANOTHER APPROACH

What does the Bible teach about this apparent state of illogic? Remarkably enough, neither the New nor the Old Testament sees any *illogic* in the situation! For example, in Romans 1, which deals with this question in detail, Paul the apostle teaches in a clear and uncompromising manner that creation doesn't show the slightest sign of contradiction in these matters. It gives only one plain line of thought: that the whole creation reveals that God is a glorious, omnipotent Creator—and nothing else. Paul says, "Because that which may be known of God is manifest in them; for God have shewed it unto them. For the invisible things of him from the creation of the world are *clearly seen,* being understood *by the things that are made* [nature], even his eternal power and Godhead; so that they are without excuse."[1]

Thus, the Bible teaches, as do many ancient sources, that when a man regards nature, he is seeing, as in a mirror, the Creator. The Bible doesn't ignore the apparent problems of war, disease, poverty, pain and chaos. It says quite a lot about these subjects and even suggests cures for some of them. But it does not see them in the light in which my professor saw them. The Bible does not think that these things cloud the issue about the Creator, as do many thinking people. Rather, it teaches that the man who regards nature as it is today and does not see the power of a glorious, invisible Godhead *in nature*—with no clouding of the issue by the mixture of good and evil we all see—that man is "without excuse" for not believing! This is surely a rather strong pill to the modern intellectual who pleads intellectual difficulties for his disbelief in God.

Adding insult to injury, the Bible goes one step further in teaching that not only should a man see the Godhead, the glorious Creator, when he sees mixed nature, but, seeing it, he should be filled with thanks to God, glorifying him for revealing his wisdom and power in the creation. So, apparently I should have told my professor that he was not only "without excuse" but also a "thankless" person—if I had been ready to give him a biblical view of himself. Somehow, I don't think he would have appreciated that! Certainly at that time I did not have the necessary maturity to say such a thing without causing a major incident—and a lot of misunderstanding.

Paul continues the argument by maintaining that a sense of wonder and reverence should fill every observer of the present confused creation. Offsetting this wonder should be a sense of our own vanity and foolishness, pervading us and all who do not see the creation in this light. Finally, all these feelings on observing God's handiwork should make the observer a "worshiper" (glorifying him as God). If I had told my professor that he had all the evidence necessary to make him fall on his knees (or face) and worship God, undoubtedly he would have thought me a lunatic.

But Paul insists that if those reactions to the creation don't take place in us, we are abusing our reasoning power. As a consequence of this abuse we shall become totally unable, in the course of time, to use our higher reasoning faculties and logical powers. Paul expresses this thought by saying our "heart" will become "darkened" and our "imagination" will become "vain." Also, he maintains that, under such circumstances, even sexual morality will die in us. Men will begin to sexually abuse their own bodies—homosexuality will arise, and normal sex relations will be stifled. Certainly my professor would not have appreciated this step of the argument in the least, for he appeared to be a moral man.

In summary, at least parts of Holy Scripture do not appear to sympathize greatly with the intellectual difficulties discussed here. The Bible says a look at nature as it is should be enough to make man a convinced, thankful, worshiping believer. The question remains: why does the Bible take this stand, seeing that at least some thoughtful modern people in the Western world today have found that the observation of the universe has by no means made them worshipers or believers. (Here I am not thinking of Taoists, etc.) On the contrary, those who have studied the universe in the natural sciences and other disciplines have often felt the most difficulties with respect to worshiping and believing. Indeed, quite a majority have simply turned away from any thought of God.

Investigation of "that which is seen" has not revealed to them "the unseen" but has often turned them from believing in anything divine and unseen. In no way has it made them worshipers of some unseen Being. For what they've seen shows so many paradoxes and apparent contradictions that, judging the unseen by what they see, it becomes either ridiculous or superfluous for further serious thought.

Since intellectuals conclude that if the seen can give no credible picture of the unseen—if there is an unseen—being a Christian is synonymous with being a third-rate intellectual. They assume that the Christian is intellectually incapable of comprehending the contradictions and paradoxes inherent in the allegedly rather naïve and intellectually impossible Christian faith.

Clearly, the basic difficulty confronting both the Christian and the intellectual in aligning matters of belief with matters of the intellect is intimately tied up with the question of the origin of evil. If we could account for the origin of evil without impugning God's omnipotence, love and holiness, then we would be able to go a long way toward solving these difficulties. A future chapter deals with this basic problem of the origin of evil.

chapter

3

Fallacies in the Atheistic and Agnostic Positions

Are there any really irreconcilable intellectual difficulties involved in believing in God, or are they only imaginary when carefully examined? I don't believe the ancients were on a lower intellectual plane than we moderns. Even though we have excelled them in technology, we see no evidence of intellectual lethargy on their part. Yet, perhaps a considerable percentage of them believed that the universe showed God's handiwork, whereas most moderns do not.

This difference in approach is not in any way a reflection on the total *intellectual* capacity of either the moderns or the ancients. Rather, it is a reflection of the increasing mass of knowledge with which every human being in every succeeding generation has to contend. An ancient could have been a master of all that was then known in the combined fields of physics, chemistry, mathematics, geometry, medicine, biology and algebra. Today the mass of knowledge is so great that no human brain can possibly cope with even a fraction of it. Therefore, a fragmentation of knowledge has occurred. But this massive increase has tended to take place in the watertight compartments of the various disciplines into which knowledge has become divided in order to fit the capacity of single brains. The result is that a synthesis of all modern knowledge is rapidly becoming less and less possible. This perfectly natural tendency has had some far-reaching consequences which must be examined before one considers the question of the origin of evil, since the two problems belong together.

Just over a century ago Darwin, Wallace and Huxley propounded the view that long time spans and chance reactions, coupled with natural selection, would account for all visible living nature without the necessity of involving the volition of any divinity. Huxley thought he could prove this with his appeal to probability laws and his famous six monkeys typing at random for millions of years on six typewriters. The mathematical formulae for the possibility of this view were bandied around and the principle was accepted as true. The natural and logical consequence of the view was that the postulate of divinity behind nature was rendered superfluous. Immense time spans plus chance and natural selection would do the work hitherto attributed to God. Thus the world of science became a world depending on chance as a direct result of the views of these men (though Darwin himself did not see that far).

The patient work of scientists simultaneously competent in several disciplines—biology, mathematics and chemistry—has been required to show that Darwin's basic assumptions were chemically, mathematically and biologically untenable.[1] The vastness of today's scientific knowledge makes it obvious that it is a rare scientist who is able to do original work in all these fields simultaneously. As a result, until recently no synthesis between the various fields had been achieved. Instead, watertight compartmentalization had developed. Biologists were unable to test the mathematics of the problem in hand, and the chemists could not critically assess the biologists' work.

The biologists announced with all due thunder that they could replace God with chance and long time spans plus natural selection. But no mathematicians sufficiently versed in chemistry and biology were forthcoming to assess mathematically and thermodynamically what the biologists were shouting about. As a result, one discipline, in this case biology, has been building on false chemical, thermodynamic and mathematical premises. There was no one to check them. The author has written elsewhere of the catastrophic development of this kind of compartmentalization of science.[2]

Thus, in ancient times learned men possessed a good, synthetic, overall view on life and the then-known universe. Although there were certainly errors, grave errors sometimes, in what they believed, yet, viewing the universe *as a whole,* they saw it as the product of an omnipotent divinity with a creative will. They knew that certain forms of order could only be attributed to personality and intelligence, and they proceeded to apply this general principle to the ordered universe.

In modern times, however, things have been drastically different in the realm of scientific and intellectual matters. It has become so difficult to synthesize knowledge to form a coherent whole that very few biologists studying Darwinism (or any other specialized subject) could check his mathematical or chemical assumptions. Thus, when Darwin and Huxley announced that living nature showed nothing of the divine in it or its origin, allegedly demonstrating their announcement with quite simple and apparently sound mathematical formulae, men who were being raised in compartmentalized knowledge simply believed them. Darwin's actual doctrine was very simple, and highly comfortable to those who considered the idea of a God to be primitive.

Therefore, ancient intellectuals with their simple but relatively synthesized knowledge attained a total view of the universe and its problems within their limited scientific knowledge. As a result, they could believe what the apostle Paul said about the universe demonstrating the nature of the Godhead. It was reasonable, simple, all-embracing and clear. It agreed with what they knew about mathematics and biology—even though the idea of spontaneous generation, then widely believed, might have offered difficulties on the question of creation.

What is not generally realized is that modern man could believe, as did the ancients, that the universe shows God's nature and still remain within the limits of all the scientific knowledge gained since ancient times—if his knowledge had not become so great that it had to be wrongly compartmentalized. For when the various compartments are carefully examined, the fact emerges that each still speaks one language today, as it did thousands of years ago: that "the heavens declare the glory of God," in spite of the mixture of good and bad.[3]

In spite of this surrounding evil and the mixed picture showing both evil and good, we can believe in a good loving, personal, holy and compassionate God behind it all. There never was any difficulty about believing he made the good. But what about the evil? Is he the author of that? *The Koran teaches that God made "the mischief of creation" too.*[4] Is God the author of the *mixed* picture? Is such a synthesis of knowledge possible?

THE GOTHIC CATHEDRAL
Before the Second World War, I often visited the huge and beautiful Gothic cathedral at Cologne on the Rhine in Western Germany. I used to admire this fine example of the architecture of many hundreds of years ago, with its graceful flying buttresses, a superb high-domed roof, its famous two towers, and the medieval stained-glass windows. Hearing the thunderous peals of organ music filling the huge edifice transported me in thought to passages such as Isaiah 6.

The more I admired the cathedral, the more I found myself admiring the architects and masons who had originated the whole structure. Over the centuries they had patiently planned and built. All the graceful lines and sturdy foundations had obviously been carefully planned by experts possessing sound knowledge of building mathematics and mechanics as well as a keen appreciation of how to combine both to produce a beautiful total edifice.

That it had so well withstood the ravages of the centuries showed that the workmen and designers not only understood the principles behind beauty, but also those of ensuring endurance. Their craftsmanship was first class in every way. Thus I found myself admiring our forefathers as I admired their workmanship. Considering that they had few mechanical devices such as a modern architect would consider essential for constructing such a masterpiece, the masons and architects of that day certainly did work wonders.

The structure of that cathedral, centuries after it had been built, showed without the slightest doubt something of the mind or minds behind it. Its very compact and organized design made one wonder what sort of drawing offices the builders had at their disposal and how they made their blueprints. To imagine that such a well-conceived edifice simply arose without enormous planning effort would be to invite the just derision of anyone remotely familiar with the construction industry. Even calculations of the strengths of the various construction materials had to be made with old-fashioned arithmetic, and not just handed over to a computer. Thus, an almost flawless work showed sharply the minds and hands of its creators. But the picture did not always remain as clear.

COMPLICATING THE ISSUE

During the war, Cologne suffered perhaps the most intensive air bombardment of any city in Western Europe. Reportedly, bombs fell on about every two square yards of the entire inner city. Now, the cathedral stands almost directly in the railroad station yard. Cologne is a very important rail center where many lines meet, particularly those connected with the huge and concentrated Ruhr industrial area. Naturally the Allies bombed the railroad yards on many occasions and, not surprisingly, many bombs missed their mark and destroyed nearby housing and property. A number of heavy bombs hit the cathedral, doing immense damage.

In the fall of 1946 when I returned to Germany for the first time after the war, I was greatly dismayed at the sight of the cathedral. It seemed symbolic of the rest of Europe and her spirit. Almost irreparable damage had been done in five years of combat. However, as I approached, the two famous towers were still visible through the morning mist.

Practically every building in the vicinity was razed to the ground; the cathedral alone stood majestically in the midst of the carnage. Coming nearer, however, I could see huge, gaping holes in the sides of the two towers. The holes revealed the massiveness of the masonry, for any other building receiving glancing blows from such high-explosive bombs would have collapsed entirely. But the cathedral, though, badly damaged, was not destroyed. Hundred of tons of concrete and bricks had been used to plug a huge hole high up in one tower, partially replacing the ancient masonry which had been blasted away by an aerial bomb.

The ancient roof was indescribably damaged. Huge rafters and beams, once its glory, hung perilously down over the bomb-pocked floor. As the wind blew through the wreckage, small bits and pieces fell to the ground, building up the piles of rubble. A hole marked the place where the organ had once pealed out its accompaniment to worship.

This miserable picture of chaos made a deep impression on me as I stood in the same place where I had once admired the order and beauty of the original edifice. As those memories of former beauty passed through my mind, one idea never even occurred to me. Never did I connect the chaos of the formerly beautiful cathedral with any inefficiency or designed purpose on the part of the constructing architects or masons! They had not constructed it for such maltreatment.

Similarly, I never began to doubt the existence of the men who designed and constructed the cathedral simply because I could now see so many contradictions in their handiwork. The place was a ruin. *But in its ruination it still bore the marks of design. In fact, its design and original beauty were even more emphasized in some respects. For the huge gaping holes in the walls revealed the excellent construction even better than did the remaining undamaged walls.* There was no fill or rubbish behind false walls, such as if found in many modern buildings. It was all solid handiwork built to last for centuries. The mighty flying buttresses were still there; the graceful Gothic arches were still standing. But the solid design which was built into the parts of the construction normally hidden from view, was now laid bare for all to see how well those craftsmen had done their job.

In summary, even the general ruin and chaos showed (1) the existence of and (2) the excellent work of both architects and craftsmen. Furthermore, the *ruined* structure itself showed in some ways even better than the intact one the existence and skill of the originators. In fact, the whole picture reminded me of the purpose of dissection in learning the anatomy of animals, man and plants. In order to see the order—and beauty—of some aspects of biology, the destroyed or dissected animal or plant serves *better than the intact one.* The cathedral had certainly been dissected, and its entrails laid bare.

INEFFICIENT ARCHITECTS?

Obviously no one was going to accuse the architects and craftsmen of designing and producing a ruin. The cathedral had been constructed to last—almost forever. Something had happened to it which had not been planned or even conceived of. And yet, even in its ruination, it was generally quite easy to distinguish between the unplanned ruin and the actual architecture. Although the cathedral at the same time displayed both perfection and ruination, certainly a mixed picture, this fact would never allow either of these conclusions: (1) that, because the cathedral was a ruin, a mixture of chaos and order, there could therefore be *no mind, no volition, no architect*, behind it; and, (2) that, because the edifice was a mixture of ruin and order, one could therefore no longer hope to recognize any *characteristics of a mind behind it.* It would not occur, surely, to anyone that one mind had planned and carried out both the construction and destruction of the edifice. That would be sheer nihilism!

The ruined cathedral presents a mixed picture—chaos and order mixed up inextricably with one another, just as the world around us presents a picture full of good and evil, beauty and ugliness, order and chaos, love and hate. No one in his right mind ought to deny that life as we see it is a hopeless hodgepodge of such ingredients. However, we should remember that it would be just as illogical to say that the mixed picture of the cathedral *proves* there was no architect behind it as to say that the ruined, mixed picture we see of life about us *proves* that there is no God behind it. My professor, rightly seeing the hodgepodge before him, concluded that *therefore:*

1. The edifice of creation has no mind or architect behind it. This is the position of all atheists who hold the same views. For the atheist maintains that because he sees nothing but contradictions in nature, therefore there is no mind or God behind it. The Germans call this a *Denkfehler,* a short circuit in the logic of thinking. And so it is. But it is one seldom seen through today.

2. No characteristics of a mind behind nature can be distinguished because the picture is so mixed. This again is a *Denkfehler* because, as we have already pointed out in the case of the ruined cathedral, *as long as any signs of order have*

escaped complete destruction in the general ruin, these "broken bits and pieces remaining of the flying buttresses and Gothic arches" will still show what sort of men planned them. Thus, even widely separated little pools of beauty, love, joy, order, healthy bodies, and virtue which are remaining in the general hate, war, destruction, chaos and ugliness of the world of nature in which we live, still point unflinchingly to the architect who designed and produced it before ruination set in.

In fact, as seen in the cathedral, when chaos replaces order, it can often dissect and lay bare the original order even better than could the intact orderliness of an organism, or unruined nature itself. The study of cancer cells—a good example of the "ruination" to which living entities can easily come—has laid bare many secrets of the healthy intact cell which would never have been even suspected had we had only normal healthy cells under our microscopes.

SUMMARY

Therefore, we can maintain that even though the creation around us is certainly a hodgepodge of good and bad, ugly and beautiful, love and hate, and even though life certainly does present a badly mixed picture, it is still untenable to conclude with my professor that this means no architect is behind it, and that it was all due to chance and long time spans and would therefore be expected to be a hopeless mess. Any little pool of love, order, kindness, beauty or design in the general rubble heap of nature must lead us to a mind or designer behind that pool, no matter how small and smothered in rubble it may be. For that pool will still unswervingly reflect its designer's character, even though representing one-thousandth of a percent of the amount of rubble. Thus, a synthesis *is* possible.

And yet, it is the position of atheists and agnostics the world over that *nothing can be known* about whether a creator exists, or what sort of character he might have, simply because the nature of the creation he made is now a mixed-up hodge-podge of good and bad. But any little tidbit of beauty or order—no matter how great the surrounding rubble—reveals the fallacy of this view. One would have thought that the illogical nature of the whole atheistic and agnostic position would have become clear long ago. The only refuge it can really try to hide behind is the modern one which Kirkegaard and the new theology have already taken, namely, that there is no such thing as a logical thought process which might be valid in such arguments. But, taking that position, we are immediately led straight to absolute nihilism in thought, so we might as well start dissecting all the gray matter from our brains so that thought itself will no longer be necessary to arrive at any conclusions!

Surely this is one reason why Romans 1 is so dogmatic. The creation, even though it is undoubtedly mixed now, being full of the rubble of hate, sin, ugliness and violence, still does show some pools of love, kindness, beauty and virtue, thereby proclaiming (1) that there is an architect behind these pools, and (2) that his very character is shown by these pools, small though they be. In fact, the Bible teaches from cover to cover that illness, death, hate and ugliness are all signs and outward manifestations of a state of "ruin" which overtook a once-better world. It also teaches that the signs of "ruin" are easily distinguished from the "pools" of order, love and virtue which still bear testimony to the state of the original edifice.

Thus, even today, the teaching of Romans 1 that the universe—even the fallen, damaged or ruined universe—when inspected reveals enough of its Maker to bring any honest-thinking, logical person to his knees in thankfulness and worship, still holds true. The surprising thing is that our forefathers, until the middle of the last century, recognized this mode of thought. Only the advent of a concept of origins of creation, *which ascribed the order we see to a spontaneous origin in chaos,* unseated the earlier views. But take away the view that order can arise spontaneously from chaos, as Darwinians and others have taught with impunity for over a hundred years and which is utterly untenable in the light of modern mathematics, physics, thermodynamics, as well as chemistry, and the older views become immediately tenable again, and indeed, unavoidable, even today. For if order—no matter how minute—did not arise spontaneously from chaos—which physics, mathematics as well as chemistry will not allow—it must have arisen in a mind. Thus we can still maintain that Romans 1 represents a true statement of fact, and that inspection of nature must lead to recognition of its Maker and his character. Atheists and agnostics are still "without excuse."

Obviously, some difficulties remain in illustrations of this type. Some of these are examined in the following chapter as we pursue our synthesis.

4

The Origin of Evil

Difficulties of the type discussed in chapter 2 led Baudelaire, the French art historian and poet, to exclaim, "If there is a God, he is the devil!" As F. Schaeffer rightly points out, such a statement is the direct result of believing that man has always been as he is, that he was so designed originally. In that case, the architect (if there is one) *designed* the mixed picture and is therefore *responsible* for designing the bad as well as the good. This is the Muslim position.

Theistic evolutionists cannot avoid the same difficulty when they maintain that God used evolutionary processes to produce the world of nature *as we see it today.* If he did, *then his methods made the bad with the good, as Baudelaire maintains, and he therefore must be the devil as well as God.* Everything pivots on whether we believe nature was once "good" and then subsequently ruined. That is, whether we believe in the fall of man as laid down in Genesis. By tampering with the structural details of Genesis, we are likely to garble the whole reason for the present state of man—and the whole plan of his salvation which will take him out of the present disastrous mess. Genesis presents an integral whole on which the total plan of Scripture is firmly founded. This includes the fact of man's fall, bringing with it the ruination of all nature with his ruin. Baudelaire's tremendous conclusion throws light not only on what art historians like himself must believe if they are logical, but also on what theistic evolutionists conclude.

Let us return to the cathedral illustration of chapter 2. It is superfluous to point out that all illustrations and analogies are imperfect and have their weaknesses if pressed too far. Our illustration of the cathedral is no exception. One of its imperfections lies in the fact that the architects who designed and built the cathedral are long-since dead and therefore could not prevent the bombing of their masterpiece. Then is God dead, too? Was he dead when his masterpiece, nature, was "bombed" into ruin?

Today many assume God to be, in fact, dead and resolve the question that way. But this is an escape exit for several reasons. Although it might explain God's creative work in the past and its subsequent ruination, it would never explain the *present maintenance* of nature and creation. Such maintenance demands, in current jargon, a full-time living maintenance service! No dead God could take care of that. Christians rightly believe that he is not only the living Creator but also the living Maintainer of nature—and of us. By very definition, the "God is dead" theory will not fit in here. For maintenance implies activity and life.

So the question now becomes: Why didn't an almighty God who made, maintains, and presumably loves his masterpiece, the creation, prevent its "bombing"? Here the parable of the cathedral can do us no more service.

People who continually ask the question, "Why doesn't God stop it?" are often those who don't bother to ask what "stopping it" would entail. Some specific details must be examined before attempting to solve the larger principles involved if God were to "stop it."

Consider any virture of which a person is capable. Love, kindness, honesty, faithfulness, chastity, or any of the virtues named in Galatians 5 will do. Select a virtue which pleases us all—love—and ask the following question: "What is the nature of love in particular, and virtue in general?"

NATURE OF LOVE AND VIRTUE

This subject of the nature of love and virtue is vitally important because the Christian way of life maintains that *God himself is love.* Christians in the Western world often do not realize the tremendous import of this statement. I have given other religions, including Islam, some thought, and have studied Islam's holy book, the Koran, which designates Allah as the compassionate, forgiving one. As far as I know, nowhere in the Koran does Allah figure specifically as an embodiment of love. He may threaten, he may be merciful, omnipotent, compassionate and omnipresent. He may offer the faithful a place in the gardens of paradise with as many dark-eyed houris as they wish.[2] But love never figures in the Koranic "revelations" of Allah's nature. A designation of God as "love" stands unique in the Bible.

Right in the center, then, of the Christian position is this virtue we call love. It must be of vital importance for that very reason. Nevertheless, I find myself at an extreme loss when I am asked to rationally explain anything at all about God's love. I know that "God so *loved* the world that he gave his only Son, that whoever believes in him should not perish but have eternal life,"[3] and I am profoundly grateful for this. But God, even though loving, is also infinite. Therefore, he exceeds anything my thinking apparatus can handle. So I do not pretend to be able to plumb the depths of either his love or character. To think rationally about *that* love is far beyond me.

I suspect it is for this reason that when the Scriptures speak of God and his love, usually man's love—particularly man's love to a woman and vice versa—is used to drive home the point at an anthropomorphic level. It is like using real-life illustrations to clarify abstract and abstruse points of chemistry to unscientific people. Thus, God provides us information on himself and his love in a human setting of human love in order to really communicate with us. The example we all understand best in human relationships—the love of a young man for his bride—can illustrate something about love in general. The information we thus obtain by "cutting down the high voltage of God's love" to the "low voltage of human love" we will then apply to our main problem.

The first question in analyzing human love is: "How did this love between bride and bridegroom originate?" The history of most such relationships provides the answer. The young man one day met the girl and sooner or later began to feel attracted to her. The attraction is better experienced than described. Very often the girl feels attracted to him at the same time, although she would at this stage probably be more hesitant to display her feelings. Normally, any open expression of this almost noncommunicable relationship springing up between the pair comes from his side, not hers. He begins the action side of the relationship by looking for suitable ways to court or woo her. But, until he begins that courting, the whole love affair is one-sided, or lopsided. A one-sided relationship in which attentions are not returned can be extremely painful. Certainly it is neither happy nor satisfying to either party.

At this stage there is one burning question which every prospective bridegroom would like answered as soon as possible: Does she love me? Is my attraction to her reciprocated? Does she feel toward me as I do toward her? One purpose of courtship is to give the girl a chance to settle the question in her own mind. For, once she notices the man's attentions and, therefore, attraction toward her, she has to make a momentous decision: Do I and can I return his affection? If she is wise, she may turn for advice to a trusted girl friend, or perhaps to her parents, who have already traveled this road and are therefore more experienced than she. If she finally thinks she may return the affection, then she must decide if she *can* love him. Here she must rely on her own heart, as well as on her common sense and the principles of life to which she adheres. After due consideration, then, she may decide she does and can return his attraction toward herself. An understanding is reached between the two. A radiant couple emerges, and great are the happiness and joy of two hearts that have entrusted themselves in mutual love and faithfulness.

In order to answer the question of why a *God of love* just doesn't "stop it" we must analyze the process of falling in love in order to draw some reason out of what often appears to be an entirely unreasonable happening.

First, the young man must *court* the girl of his choice. She will be unhappy if he doesn't, and he will be unmanly if he doesn't know how! Now, courtship is a very fine art, besides being a very necessary one. Some of our finest poetry, music and art have arisen as by-products of this art! Most important, perhaps, is that it is a so-called *gentle art,* which brings us to a cardinal point in our analysis.

The moment *force* takes the place of *wooing,* both love and the joy of love cease. They are often replaced by hate, recriminations and misery. For the whole structure of love is built on absolute *mutual consent* and respect for the sovereignty of the person and character of the loved one. In other words, the structure on which human love between a bride and bridegroom is squarely based is *freedom to love*—mutual consent or absolute free will on the part of both partners to give one another their entire and exclusive affection.

Most civilized societies recognize precisely this structure in their marriage services. The two persons intending marriage are both given the public opportunity of making a free-will consent in saying "I will" before the assembled congregation. Old

Testament cultures stand for exactly the same principle, as the following well-known history emphasizes.

REBEKAH

When Eliezer, Abraham's servant, asked Rebekah to become Isaac's wife (Gen. 24), he became so assured that he had found God's choice for his master's son that he was ready to cut corners in the process of taking the bride home. The evidence that Rebekah was God's choice was so overwhelming that he wanted to speed things up so he could take her home triumphantly. He just wanted to take off immediately with the girl and forget about all the formalities or ceremonies.

However, Rebekah's relatives saw immediately that this was no basis for marriage, even though the Lord might be in it. What a good thing it would be if young couples saw this point too, instead of just starting to live together with no ado and ceremonies. It is to emphasize the necessity of mutual public consent before love and lifelong married joy, the greatest relationship in our earthly life, that Rebekah's relatives got together and said that even though God might be in it all, Rebekah must first be publicly questioned on the matter. She had to give her own opinion and decision before they would let her go to Isaac. So they called her in before the family and their friends to ask her whether she wanted Isaac. Only after she had given her public consent, based on her own free-will decision, did they agree to the marriage. They knew that no other basis was good enough, even though it was obviously God's will even without such public decision-making.

THE AMNON AND TAMAR AFFAIR

Thus, the first point arising out of this analysis of the basis of bride-bridegroom relationships and love is that such a partnership is based firmly on public mutual consent or free will.

The second point deals with the consequences of neglecting the above point. The shocking "love affair" between Amnon and Tamar (2 Sam. 13) illustrates this danger in a crass way. Amnon fell madly in love with the king's beautiful daughter Tamar. He was so infatuated with the fair girl that he just could not wait to woo her and win her consent. As a result, what could have made an excellent love story became a scandal to the whole royal court.

By guile Amnon arranged to be alone with the girl. Feigning sickness, he received the king's permission for Tamar to come and cook for him in his apartment. Having gotten rid of everyone else, he proceeded to force the poor girl because he was so madly "in love" with her. "Love" that cannot wait to woo is abnormal. It often metamorphoses before our eyes into what we call "lust."

The consequence of this haste and trickery was that Amnon's "love" turned in a twinkling into hate for her. He brutally threw the weeping and brokenhearted Tamar out of his room, bolting the door behind her. The eventual result was murder, for her relatives had Amnon murdered later for his brutality and treachery. Of course, Tamar suffered terribly under the shame and heartbreak, and she "remained desolate in her brother Absalom's house" (2 Sam. 13:20).

FREE CHOICE

Therefore, in order to *love* in this sense—not merely physical union, which can result from mere lust—we must experience the mutual attraction and union of body, soul and spirit in an exclusive personal relationship. Mere physical union, if not accompanied by the corresponding union of that whole trinity, plus the personality, of which man and woman consist, brings a travesty of the laws of nature governing the relationships between a bride and her bridegroom. The practice of the union of the female body with the male, with nothing else involved, reduces man to a beast. Whoredom sears his whole psyche and causes many problems of the mind. A large percentage of mental illness can be traced to such practices.

Today, because the physical consequences are easily dispensed with since no children need result, intercourse on this basis is perhaps more widely practiced than ever before—with ever increasing psychic illness.

If the basis of mutual consent in the love relationship is removed, if there is *no freedom to love,* if freedom is replaced by force, then all possibility of loving is removed. Love can be replaced then by its opposite—hate. In other words, to be able to really love there must be genuine freedom to love. This implies, of course, the further step of logic: where there is true freedom to love, there is also true freedom *not to love.* For, if this freedom to say no were not really present, there would ipso facto be no freedom to say yes and to love. The "no" or the ability to say no, must be just as genuine as the ability to say yes if true mutual consent is to be achieved, which is the basis of the whole structure of the love of a man for his bride.

As we have seen, the Bible teaches that God himself is love, and his love is often likened to the bride-bridegroom relationship. Our third conclusion is that if his love to us is to be compared in some way with our human nuptial love, then the principles governing the two loves can be expected to be comparable in some ways. We should expect God, on this basis, to be the grand wooer. That being the case, we should expect him to be looking for our response to his wooing. To receive and experience his love we should expect the *mutual-consent basis to decide everything*—my consent to him in answer to his "attraction to and love for" me.

Thus, we conclude that if God is love in this sense of the word, he will be looking for *answering love* from me. Love is only satisfied if it is answered or returned. He woos us by many means, mainly by having sent his Son, the second Person of the Trinity, to justify us by dying and being resurrected for us.

Being love, we would not expect him to demand or attempt to force love. That would be a contradiction. The very attempt

63

to do so would destroy the very basis of all love. As our true lover he does everything to show the genuine nature of his love—even to becoming a fellowman, heir to our lot as well as bearing our sin. In keeping with his character of love, Jesus, of his own free will went to the cross to demonstrate that his love to fallen man was no flash in the pan. He was serious about it—serious even to death. Greater love has no man than that he lay down his life for his friend. In his efforts at wooing mankind, Jesus Christ went further than that, for he lay down his life for the very people who demonstrated themselves to be his enemies by crucifying him. This all fits in with his character when it is described as being that of love.

THE CASE OF THE ROBOT

Consider one more vital point. What would have happened if God had so constructed man that he could not make a true free-will decision himself, but was capable only of automatically doing God's will, just as a lock opens when one turns the correct key in it? Or just as an automatic vending machine delivers the bar of chocolate when one inserts the correct coin. If man had been so constructed that, when a certain "button" in his mind was depressed he delivered "love" just as automatically as when the coin sets off the mechanism of the vending machine and delivers the cup of coffee, would love—real love—be in fact delivered? If we were constructed like marionettes, complete with strings, the pulling of certain strings would make us go through definite motions which might resemble the outward "motions" of love. But could a marionette *love*? Is it capable of love? Of course the answer is negative, simply because a marionette is not a person with all a person's dignity of free will. The fact that it is not endowed with the qualities belonging to a person, such as free will, make it incapable, "congenitally" incapable, of love. This is simply because it cannot say or mean either "yes" or "no" in any real sense of the word. It has no will, no personality, and therefore is not capable of any *virtues*, least of all the virtue called love.

None of us would be interested in "loving" the outward form of a partner who, every time we touched a certain "button," put chocolate in its mouth or stroked its hair, and automatically intoned the sentence, "I love you." In fact, could any system be so constructed as to deliver any "virtue" on command? If such a system were conceived or constructed, it would have to be subhuman or machine by nature. For to try to construct it so that it delivered "virtue" or "love" *on command* would of necessity mean that it be devoid of humanity, and therefore personality, and as a result it could deliver nothing of the kind. Assume that God, *in order to be sure of our love* and to make sure that we were "virtuous" in every way, made us like marionettes. He would have taken from us the possibility of really exercising our free will in order that we could not exercise it wrongly. Wanting to be so sure that we loved him and our fellowmen, he would have made us so that we could not do otherwise. Whenever he presses the button, we would "deliver the goods" just like a vending machine. Could such a setup involve real love in any way?

THE GRAND RISK

This brings us right up to the great principle. If God wanted creatures that really loved him and their fellow creatures, he was, by the very intrinsic nature of love, obliged to recognize the truth (though it sounds strange to use such phraseology and maintain that God was *forced* to do anything his own moral nature brings with it the consequence that he will or must act according to that nature) that love and virtue demand freedom, absolute freedom, to love and exercise virtue. Otherwise there could be neither love nor freedom. Such a necessity lies in the very structure of love and, indeed, of *any other true virtue*. Thus, to create the possibility of love, God had to create *free personalities* just like himself, for he is love and made us to love.

For God to plan at all for true love involved the built-in risk of the proposed free partner in love not loving at all. *To have built the love partner so that he would be "congenitally" obliged to respond would have been to destroy the whole purpose of designing a creation where love could reign.* God wished—and still wishes—to set up a *kingdom of love* on earth and in heaven. But to do so involves the above-outlined risk of the free partners choosing not to love, but to do the opposite, of their own free will—and not respond to love by being indifferent to the divine wooing—or even hating. The practical result of being indifferent to or hating is the same from the divine partner's point of view. For there is no positive *response* to his love in either case. And love aims at a response of love. Thus, love either grows by responding, or it dies.

The risk involved in planning a creation where love could reign is a built-in risk. It is the risk of wooing not being responded to, the risk of the proposed partner not loving back in response. It is usually that class of person who does not consider implications of this kind who is always so keen on having God play the role of the "dictator" and use brute force to "make things better." Of course, he could if he wanted to. He is omnipotent; he is Lord. "Allah" tends to be this type of lord. But, although the Christian God is just and sees the wrongs to be righted, they will always be righted in the light of the fact that he is love—right up until the day of judgment dawns.

ALMSGIVING AND THE SOCIALIST STATE

Exactly the same risk is involved in planning every and any virtue. Take, for example, the virtue of almsgiving. In Turkey one sees hundreds of needy beggars. There are the blind holding their certified photographs of their suffering wives and children who need support. There are those lying in the gutters, with their misshapen bodies uncovered so that all who pass by can see they are not counterfeiting. There is the poor man who has feet where his knees should be, loudly and slowly repeating selected passages from the Koran. There is the old man suffering from Parkinsonianism, whose saliva continually runs over his poor old dirty face as he holds out an empty trembling hand all day long. Seeing this misery causes one to exercise compassion and give a coin so that they can eat a slice of good Turkish bread. Naturally one is convinced that something much more fundamental should be done for these thousands of people so representative of suffering humanity. But a coin will at least guarantee that the immediate plague of gnawing hunger will be assuaged.

So one gives something to the young mother sitting in rags underneath the mailbox at the post office, with her week-old unwashed baby on her ragged lap. In so doing one exercises a virtue—that of almsgiving. The immediate reward is an extra-fervent prayer to Allah for the giver's salvation. The joy on the recipient's face would be reward enough. To exercise any virtue is a free-will operation which brings joy to the giver and to the receiver.

If, however, beggars are cared for by taxes, and if the city authorities send me a tax bill to help support the poor and needy, then I must pay. It is my duty. It may be a good thing to organize matters in this way. Many maintain that this method is less degrading for the poor, and that the burden is more equally distributed. I agree with them, as far as they go. But let us be clear about one of the overlooked consequences.

In paying my taxes which are used to support the poor and needy, I no longer exercise the virtue I did when I gave the alms to the poor young mother. I might have paid about $10 in taxes for the poor, or I might have given the poor young woman $10 to buy her baby something better than dirty rags. The sum of money actually involved makes little difference. In one case I exercise the virtue of almsgiving (and reap a blessing) while in the other case I pay my taxes and do my duty, grumbling perhaps about the waste perpetrated by the bureaucrasy of the tax office, with no consequent blessing, even though I may be perfectly right.

In one case I exercise no virtue, even though the poor man or woman may receive exactly the same sum of money from me by way of the city authorities. In the other case, where I give of my own free will in almsgiving, I may give exactly the same sum of money, but I exercise a virtue—simply because I do not *have* to act. Therein lies the difference: in the one case, having to do one's duty and pay taxes; and in the other, not being obliged to do anything, and therefore being able to exercise a virtue. *What it means is simply that forced "charity" is no charity—and forced "love" is no love.* Love and virtue melt in the grip of force just as ice melts under the pressure of a vice.

If I force my children to be "good" when we are out visiting, they may be outwardly exemplary—sometimes they are! I am thankful for this, but I recognize the fact that most fathers will be familiar with—that this "goodness" may not be even skin-deep. Force itself, unaided, can make no one *good.* It cannot make anyone exercise a virtue. This is not saying anything at all against the use of force as a punishment in education or wrongdoing. Here force may be the only solution and the only corrective. But in itself it does not make anyone good, and virtues tend to melt away in its presence.

These considerations disclose one of the fatal weaknesses of our increasingly socialized world. All "charity" and "works of love" tend to become organized by the state, which rightly wishes to eliminate the humiliation to which the poor are subjected in accepting certain kinds of "charity." Some unfortunate people do give, either to build up a mythical bank balance in heaven, or even to humiliate those who receive their money. But, no matter what ends are in view, acts of pure charity are abolished, to be replaced by the compulsion of taxes and state "relief." The joy and virtue of true charity and love disappear immediately when the forced tax replaces the free-will offering. The Lord Jesus Christ himself remarked that it was more blessed to *give* than to receive, thus emphasizing the "blessedness" or happiness accompanying the free act of giving.

The exercise of any virtue ennobles and enriches the character, giving real joy and radiance to him who exercises it, whereas the mere unwilling taxpayer may pay his taxes because he must. He often does so begrudgingly because he knows a large amount is wasted in bureaucracy, which fact and state of mind exclude the élan of the "freeman" who in his freedom nourishes his character and mind on the happiness accompanying the exercise of love. Thus the socialized state often robs its citizens of the flights of exuberance to which free exercisers of love and charity are heir.

GEORGE MÜLLER'S ORPHANAGES

Over a century ago in Bristol, England, George Müller set up his orphan homes which were run and staffed entirely by the free-will offerings and services of Christians in sympathy with his aims. Witnesses of Müller's work said that those homes full of the victims of suffering were real havens of love, joy and rest to thousands of orphans. Today many such orphanages (not Müller's) have been taken over by the state. The state institute is often merely a matter of rates and taxes, and the person in charge is sometimes a career person who makes no attempt to be a "mother" or "father" to the children. Often the atmosphere of such an institution is as cold and devoid of love as the concrete bricks of which it is constructed. Scientists have shown that children in such institutions die from lack of love as often as they die from disease.[4]

The welfare state, in taking over everything to remove a few real abuses, too often kills love and the other virtues which make up the atmosphere of a home. Removing the freedom of service, the voluntary basis, causes love to evaporate. Not only do the children or other inmates of such institutions suffer. The ennobling of character which the staff members would themselves receive by free-will service is lost by their too becoming merely career people. *The more the world loses this right to freely exercise true charity, the harder, colder and more bitter it must get.* Too few people will be in the process of receiving ennoblement of character by exercise of their freedom to do good.

This disastrous effect on the character of modern nations is nowhere more clearly seen than in the most socialized and organized nations. The motive behind the socialization was, without a doubt, entirely good. It was that of organizing poverty out of this world. As such, we must recognize the motivation to have been thoroughly good. But its mode of operation is robbing our civilization of warmhearted personal care and love. In fact, it is producing everywhere just what Hitler produced in Germany by the same means: depersonalization—people who may do their duty but who will not raise a finger to help close a concentration camp if it involves personal risk. Their characters have not experienced the ennobling, strengthening effect which results from the exercise of freedom. Hitler was a living example of a man who was naïve enough to attempt to *demand* and *command* the love and affection of his people. He may have realized at the end that love evaporates under just such a pressure. The strength of character necessary to withstand any tyrant is not likely to be built in any generation without the ennoblement of character resulting from long exercise of the various human virtues we have discussed. Such strength will also overcome the various vicissitudes of life which often complicate the career of anyone strong enough in will to be ready to suffer for his own conscience's sake.

The tendency today in most modern socialized states is to take away any private opportunity or initiative for the exercise of private virtue, and to push everything onto the community. This results in private character impoverishment. We all know the person who "doesn't want to get involved." The second tendency, contingent partly on the first, is to bring up every child to conformity so that only the will of the community and majority counts. Unfortunately, the majority is not always right. Thus the steel of a private conscience, independent of conformity to the mass, does not develop. In Hitler's Germany this was seen at its extreme development. People saw corpses drop out of vans coming from a concentration camp as they passed through a big city. But fear had so eroded characters that no one did anything—it was too dangerous to get involved!

In Chicago two years ago as I was walking from the Chicago and North Western Railway Station I saw a man in a car literally plow his way through a group of old ladies as they crossed the street on a pedestrian crossing with the green light. He knocked one old lady down, injuring her. I took the license number of the car, which did not stop, and asked for witnesses. Many young men and women going to work in a neighboring shoe factory had seen the incident. But all backed away, muttering something about not getting involved. I didn't get a single witness.

The idea of the community providing for everyone's need "from the cradle to the grave" may be excellent from purely a humanitarian point of view. But, insofar as it takes away personal initiative, the realization of the scheme will never provide sterling characters ready and willing to suffer for conscience's sake and to stand alone, if necessary. For the whole scheme erodes character.

THE CREATION, SEEN AND UNSEEN

The Bible reports that when God contemplated the creation of the worlds seen and unseen he wished to construct them so that they reflected his very own nature and character. To do this, he had to build on freedom of action. He is free, so he made man and angels free too. Man was made "in his image"— that is, as a free personality, just as God himself is. For even "his *service* is perfect freedom" and therefore founded and maintained in love. Accordingly, the angels who serve him, including their chief, Lucifer, the light-bearer, were given natures capable of genuine love to their Creator and toward their fellows. They were capable of wooing his love and being wooed by him so that the perfect joy of love could reign in that kingdom. But this very possibility of a perfect, joyous, loving kingdom had to include the possibility of the rejection of both. There were no puppets.

The Bible reports, quite as a matter of fact, that a large proportion of that unseen host showed that it really was capable of the joy of that kingdom of love and—by a very real proof—by rejection! Therefore, Lucifer did, in fact, show that he could love, in that he began, for reasons of pride, to reject the one perfect lover, his Creator. *Turning his back on him who is the sole good,* he became the epitome of the bad. So arose the cursed, loveless and hateful ones who, in the exercise of their characters, now turned away from the good toward the bad, and proceeded to "bomb" and destroy the good earth, the good creation. Men become "devils" by exactly the same process. Obviously God, his nature being love, did not immediately take away all freedom of action and choice from his creatures, thus removing the possibility of a *return to love.* He allowed them still further freedom of choice, which meant, in their case, still further "bombing" activities being permitted. If he had taken away this possibility of freedom of choice at the first sign of rejection of love, he would have destroyed any further possibility of a return to love. So he has given us all a long time of freedom of action, that is, freedom to love, so that the kingdom of love can still begin again to rule, if man and angel want it. *To "have stopped it all" at once by the strong hand of "dictatorship" would have automat-*

ically destroyed the very purpose for which the Creator had created his universe—in order to set up a kingdom of love in the seen and the unseen.

Therefore, this very existence of evil in a world created by an almighty but also a loving God actually illustrates that the good and the virtue within it really are genuine, bona-fide good. Love in such a kingdom really is love and not anything else. Sometimes it is taught that love is a covert form of egoism, etc. The state of our fallen world really shows this to be impossible—the love of God in a world of blood is genuine enough!

Destroyers and haters usually want company in their activities. So when the chief, Lucifer the light-bearer, had become the destroyer and the hater, he immediately approached Eve to make her and her husband become a part of his company of destroyers. The pair was also capable of true love. They possessed true freedom of choice, as is shown by the actual choice they made. They too turned their backs on the good, the only good, automatically becoming polarized to the bad, the chronically bad. So the whole seen and unseen creation of love became a creation of the wrong choice—the choice which turned its back on the source of all ultimate good. In leaving open a chance for seen and unseen creation to return to the ultimate good, God did not "stop the bad." The free choice was still left open, leaving the ruination and its cause still intact. *And that is the reason why God allows it—to give a genuine chance for the return of love in general.*

THE DIGNITY OF MAN

But does not all this lead to one main conclusion? Does it not all go to show the truly high esteem in which God holds his creatures, man included? It means that God really takes our decisions, our thoughts, and ourselves seriously. He even goes to the length of wooing us to make our decisions ourselves. He does not so construct us that we are puppets who have all decisions preprogramed—even though many physical processes in the body are preprogramed.[5] True love is, in this respect, always the same—it always *esteems* and *respects* its partner. It takes the partner seriously.

The same thought also expresses why God bothers to woo men by "the foolishness of preaching"[6] and not by sending, as he could, mighty angels or superintelligent creatures from other regions with his message. Perhaps they would only succeed in terrifying poor humanity if they appeared in their supernal splendor. God's purpose is *to win man's simple trust and confidence,* to win our devotion and genuine love. Therefore, he uses the natural methods available to win our decision for him. If he overawed us in any way, that might make craven slaves of us rather than wholehearted sons. If he were to browbeat us into submission, he would only gain what Hitler did—the abject, groveling fear (if not secret hatred) of his would-be partners.

Thus a God of love avoids like the plague the dictator's methods in dealing with man, the object of his love, and uses the lover's better method. *It is very fundamental to see that one cannot terrorize people into love.* Consider the miracles Jesus performed in this light. He never used a show of divine power in healing to frighten people into belief. In most cases after doing some mighty healing deed which gave sight to the blind or life to the dead, he admonished those who had seen the deed or experienced it to keep very quiet about it. Jesus' warning "tell no man" is almost proverbial in this respect. The fact is, God does not wish to force our intelligence or our will to bend us to the state of cringing slaves. He wants redeemed sons who, of their own free will, love, respect and gladly serve him.

THE DEGREE OF MAN'S FREEDOM

Thus we conclude that man must be free indeed if he is ever to be able to love indeed. There is a consequence to all this which the reader will have surely noted already. It is this: Is man so free that God has abrogated all *authority* over him? Can man do exactly and precisely as he likes as long as he likes so that he can be said to possess a totally unfettered freedom in all directions as far as he himself choses? Need he never fear that his Creator will intervene and fetter him—all in the interests of man's ability to love and exercise virtue?

Although the Bible teaches that man has a bona-fide free will and can certainly say no to his Creator's will and plan (the very state of our poor world shows that this is *de facto* the case), yet it teaches too that there are limits to that freedom just as there are limits to God's wooing activities of man. These wooing limits, it will be remembered, were founded in God's counsel from his side and, in time, from man's side. In the first place, God in his inscrutability sets a time limit for his wooing of our free will. Thus it cannot be said that we have perfect free will to accept or reject his wooing *at any time.* Our free will interacts with his free will to woo us; and if he chooses to stop the courting process, our free will can do precisely nothing about the new situation. Here it is no longer unfettered. Second, the repeated rejection of the goodness of God's courting sears the psyche of man and makes it less and less receptive. This, too, is a process we cannot alter; it is like the second law of thermodynamics at work in our inward man, and our free will cannot alter it.

The same principle applies throughout man's kingdom in its relationship to man's Creator. Man can say no to his Creator for a certain time by expressing free will. But this process of our saying no of our own free will to God interacts with God's free will and may produce a no from his side. For us dependent creatures this is the same thing as judgment supervening after grace. We all can turn our back on him and run away from him and his goodness—until we reach what may be looked upon as the end of our tether. The tether represents the change in God from grace of judgment. How long that may take in each individual case of God's dealings is unknown to his creatures. This state of affairs is well seen in the case of the apostle Paul when he was on the Damascus road and filled with hatred toward Christ and his followers. Paul had enjoyed perfect unfettered free will to rebel against Christ, and had done so very successfully, until even he reached the end of the tether God had allowed him. Then God intervened severely, blinded him, and reduced him to the dependence of a child in his helplessness. But even in a drastic intervention of this type, the judgment of God was mixed with great mercy and it led to Paul's seeing the grace of God in restricting his field of unfettered free will. But perhaps his free will in the strictest sense of the term was not touched. Perhaps his *knowledge* was increased.

If we do not recognize some definite limits to our freedom, we risk abrogating God's ultimate authority and, indeed, sovereignty. *Yet these limits in no way alter the conclusions we have drawn about the vital nature of freedom if we are to be able to love—or to rebel.* One reason for this fact is that *we ourselves do not know where the limits we are talking about lie.* Since we have no idea at all where they lie, we are, to *all intents and purposes, unlimited ourselves in our freedom viewed from our own perspective.* From our own point of view we are free to act, wander, decide, rebel or love as under-sovereigns within a small area of God's sovereign kingdom. And it is just within this area of real unrestricted freedom that real love and virtue can and do rule in us. For, not knowing any limits that have been secretly set for us, *we are free in the total areas of life known to us.* Outside these unseen limits are areas of judgment and no-freedom. But since they are unknown to us, they are, for practical purposes, *fictitious for us* and thus of no concern in our decisions to rebel or to love. The fact that God knows these limits does not impair our freedom within the area known to and experienced by us. Thus the fact of these divine limits does not in any way mar true human freedom to exercise the right to respond or reject the divine courtship. Man's freedom is all he knows until he suddenly (and mostly unexpectedly) stumbles up against the divine wall which limits us and establishes the divine sovereignty in its totality.

The very fact that man has never succeeded in devising a formal proof of God's existence, shows how completely God can and does hide himself and his limits from our eyes. This being the case, most men act within the area of their own lives as completely free agents as far as their intelligence is concerned. This makes their decisions in that frame of mind completely free will and therefore valid from the point of view exercising true virtue. We conclude, then, that the limits God has set for all mankind, do not alter our decisive free will and its accompanying power of love or rebellion. And these very limits maintain God's sovereignty while allowing man free agency in the area of his own conscious life as a mortal.

One thing more deserves mention at this point. The "tether" we have referred to as God's restricting hand on our free will should not be regarded as something fixed or static. It is not of a set permanent "length." It is my belief that the more devoted a man is to God's will for him, the longer the "tether" will become. That is, the greater will be the radius of freedom of action. To stick to our analogy of a tether, we might say that its elasticity depends upon our will being congruent with his divine will. To use the words of the apostle Paul, to "win Christ" and to attain to his confidence in us is the same thing as saying that the more we attain to the width, depth and breadth of God's will, the more we attain to his sovereign freedom too. As one prayer book has it, *"His service is perfect freedom."*

5

The Problem of Rebuilding

Just what would we expect a God of love to do after his creatures had taken the wrong road—turning their backs on the only good? Once the "bombing" of his creation had occurred, what steps would we expect him to take?

The Scriptures say that even before the wrong choice had been taken either by man or angels, God, because he is omniscient, knew all about it. He had even drawn up careful plans in advance to cope with the situation that would arise, even though he was in no sense responsible for it, nor did he cause it (cf. Rev. 13:8; Eph. 1:4; Heb. 4:3; 1 Pet. 1:19-20).

This last fact—that God, if he is God, must obviously have been omniscient with respect to the fall long before it happened—has been a stumbling block to many. Actually, few real intellectual difficulties are involved in this matter if it is considered carefully.

If I observe a person very carefully during a period of time, I may notice some of his little idiosyncrasies. He may say "Ah," for example, as a prelude to every difficult word he has to pronounce. Or he may twitch his eyebrows (or his ears) before relating a good joke. Gradually I learn to predict just what he is going to do before he actually does it. My previous observations allow me to do this with a fair amount of accuracy.

However, my ability to *foretell* his actions in no way makes me *responsible* for them when he acts. Similarly, the fact that God was able to *foresee* what Adam and Eve, the angels and mankind in general, would do, does not necessarily implicate him in the sense that it makes him *responsible* for initiating their actions and choices. The only implication is that involved in his having given them a gloriously free choice of action in order to have the possibility of their love. So God certainly foresaw the fall of both angels and man. He foresaw it so well that he made careful preparations for it, even before the very foundation of the world (Rev. 13:2). Yet, many imagine that this foreknowledge, the result of his very omniscience, must of necessity implicate God in the *guilt* of the fall. Quite the contrary, the genuine possibility of free choice which he conferred upon us in order to construct us in his image (he is the great, free superperson) so that we would be persons too, capable of really loving and exercising genuine virtue, decides forever the creatures' guilt and Creator's love and righteousness.

THE PROBLEM OF THE CONSEQUENCES

At this point many will maintain that, if God saw in advance the chaos, misery and suffering which would certainly follow the gift of the possibility of love (involving free choice) why did he proceed with his plans to create if they would result in the creation of such a miserable universe? Was he not rather sadistic to have persisted in those plans, knowing the consequences in advance? Would it not have been better to have ditched the plan if it was all going to work out as it has?

In principle the *same type* of questioning arises every day in our own lives, but seemingly we don't recognize the fact. Consider, for example, the decision we must make on whether to marry. Even the marriage ceremony emphasizes rather drastically that the same question is involved, for the clergyman says our marriage vows are binding us until *death do us part.* Surely there is scarcely greater grief than that experienced by a really devoted couple when separated by death. We *could,* of course, avoid this terrible grief by the simple expedient of not creating a marriage relationship at all! Avoid marriage and its love relationship and no grief of parting by death will ever overtake you.

Yet, we rightly go into marriage with our eyes open. We know that, in normal circumstances, death and all its sorrows *will* overtake us and *will* separate us. Most of us fear this more than we could ever say. *In spite of all this, we marry because we believe that the joy of love and the ennoblement of giving ourselves to another in the abandon of devotion even for a day (and forty or fifty years pass like a day) is better than no love at all.* It is written of Jesus Christ that he endured the sorrows of the death on the cross for the sake of the joys which would result from that sorrow.[1] The same *principle* is involved here. The joy of love, even "short" love, because it stems from a God of love, compensates for even the sorrow of a cruel death such as that which Jesus suffered for all mankind, and the death which will separate all lovers.

The enrichment and the ennoblement of the human character brought about by the experience of even the brief joy of love, as God intended it to be, compensate for the certain future death, separation, and present trials. It is a question of balance. Those who know the love of God in Christ and those who have experienced just a faint taste of that same quality of love in God-given marriage will confess that it is worth the certain severe suffering which it brings with it. *The principle is that even a little, short-lived love is better than none at all.* A few days of love—even at the price of the disaster of separation and ceasing of mortal love—is worth more than none at all.

The reason is that even mortal love changes the *eternal* human psyche. A man takes the psyche changed by love with him when this life is over and keeps it forever.

Evidently the Creator, being love personified, thinks this way too, for he *did* indeed create us and the rest of the fallen creation, in spite of the foreseen mess and separation. Although we experience many trials and tribulations, he obviously knew that the love which we can and do experience—even for a short time—more than balances the scales. Love even for a day imprints itself eternally on our psyche and is, obviously, in his eyes worth more than no love at all, which would have resulted if he had desisted from creating us free, for fear of the consequences of the foreseen fall. We will leave our trials and sufferings behind us at death, but we will forever possess the richness of love in our character. So, whichever way we look at the question of the decision to create, we must decide that, from the standpoint of love or no love, it was worth it. After all, we cannot really blame God for having created and risked the chaos, suffering and anguish in which the world finds itself, when we, in essence, make the same decision when we marry. It is the same type of decision when we have children.

All the same, many people—sometimes including ourselves —feel tempted to say "God, forgive God"[2] when contemplating the dire mess in which the world finds itself. Yet, if it is true, as the Scriptures assure us,[3] that temporal sufferings can and do bring eternal recompense, if it is true that suffering and anguish are not necessarily *punitive* but can be *remedial* as well, then, relying on the Scriptures, we are able to accept the anguish, just as God did when he crucified God to *remedy* the fall of man. This question is examined further in chapter 5.

The next question is: What would we expect God to do to pull us out of the mire?

THE PROBLEM OF GOD'S ANSWER

Now that the fall has taken place and sin and anguish are in the world, what would we expect God's answer to be? The answer we give will depend entirely on our conception of God's character. Remembering that our premise is that God is love, let us ask ourselves what we would expect such a God to do about the mess in which creation finds itself.

If God is a God of love, then he is our loved one. What would we expect a true loved one to do who had been misunderstood and rejected? Perhaps the scriptural answer is the best one here: Love "suffereth long, and is kind . . . is not easily provoked, thinketh no evil . . . beareth all things . . . endureth all things . . . [love] never faileth."[4]

Surely that is the reaction we'd expect of someone who truly loves us. Love is long-suffering, it is kind, it is not easily provoked. it endures all things in the hope of *ultimate success in the wooing process of love.* God saw man's wrong choice, and all of its consequences which would lead to chaos and anguish, long before the wrong choice was made. When it did come, however, we would not expect a real God of love to impatiently and disgustedly dismiss and destroy the object of his love. Many who have difficulties with these points apparently expect God to act like a hard-hearted, unforgiving tyrant rather than a forgiving father. Such an expectation probably arises from the fact that such action is typical of short-fused people like ourselves. But, then, we are no examples of real love in being short-fused.

In actual fact, we would expect a God of love to try to salvage what he could out of the carnage. It takes the patience of genuine love to set about this process. He had warned in faithfulness and sternness of the consequences of the wrong choice—men would surely die of it—but neither angel nor man heeded. One thing God would not be expected to do, once the wrong choice had been taken, would be to block the way back to himself—our heart's love—by attempting to threaten, cajole, or force us back. Force cannot restore anything in the way of love. That would be to cut off all possibility of a way back.

HOW TO RESTORE LOVE

Thus, in order to restore to love, there remains only one way open—the exercise of further patient love. Accordingly, God exercises long-suffering and patience in trying to win us freely back to love and reason. This same process culminated in the sending of his own Son to lay down freely his life for us all.

Therefore, we should expect a God of love, confronted by the situation in which we find ourselves, to patiently wait and quietly woo, or attempt to woo, us back. We should expect the consequences of the fall, then, not to be "fire and thunder," but rather the "still, small voice" in the attempt to realize the word said about God by the apostle: "Who desires all men . . . to come to the knowledge of the truth."[5]

But this attitude of quietness and perseverance can be mistaken for passivity or even inactivity. A large part of the Scriptures is devoted to just this point, in fact. God is not inactive; he is not indifferent. He is certainly not dead: "The Lord is not slack concerning his promise, as some men count slackness; but he is longsuffering to usward, not willing that any should perish, but that all should come to repentance."[6] This means just what it says. It does not mean that all men will repent and come to a knowledge of the truth. But it confirms that God is a God of love and patience who is ready and willing to receive *all* who do turn to him.

The fact, then, that he has waited so long after the "bombing" of his handiwork before judging the "bombers," both the original one and those who have carried on the same work in every generation (which includes me) is, in reality, another indication of God's true character—loving-kindness, patience, long-suffering, not being easily provoked. Only by looking at the situation in this way can I see any explanation of why God, the almighty, omniscient, omnipresent, righteous one, has not long since exercised withering, general judgment on all of us and set up a "puppet state" on earth and in heaven to slavishly and immediately carry out his every command, just as every dictator would do, if he could, particularly if his will had been thwarted as God's will certainly has been.

THWARTING GOD'S WILL

Some will feel shocked. Can, then, God's will be thwarted? The fatalistic Muslims think not. Is it possible that his will may not be done on earth as it is in heaven? Anyone who is not sure about this point should ask himself whether God planned any act of sadism that has taken place. Was it his will to kill six or seven million Jewish men, women and children in gas chambers for no other reason than that they were Jews? Those poor people were ordered to strip themselves naked, fold their clothes, put their shoes neatly on the floor, and then were told in four or five languages that coffee and cookies would be served them "after their communal bath." Then they were forced into a room fitted with nozzles to deliver prussic acid instead of water directly onto their naked bodies. Any children who had been forgotten in the crowd were thrown in through the windows, only openable from outside, even after the gassing had started. Often the screams lasted for fifteen minutes after the slaughter had begun. Was that not thwarting God's perfect will? And does not any other sin also thwart it?

Sinning is one way of thwarting his will. Another way would be to set up a dictatorship to "restore order to the chaotic creation." If this route to rebuilding the creation were adopted, it would just as effectively thwart God's real purpose of setting up a kingdom of love. Under the present circumstances of freedom to do good or bad there are still a few men who see the situation as it really is and who turn to God to be refreshed by his love, even in the midst of the general anguish of creation. Even a little of such love and refreshment is better than none at all. If the Lord had judged immediately after the fall or after any other sin, how many who have since drunk of the water of the well of life and love would have been lost to him and his kingdom of love forever? His *patience* has been rewarded with responding love which would have been impossible if immediate judgment had supervened.

KING GEORGE VI OF ENGLAND

A story is told about King George VI of Great Britain and how he won Elizabeth. As a young man the future king fell in love with the charming young Scottish lady. After a long time of reflection he plucked up his courage and approached her on the subject, although he was rather shy, especially with the opposite sex. He had never been much of a lady's man and was neither very robust nor strongly masculine in the film-star sense of the word. Moreover, he had a slight speech defect, which added to his difficulties. His proposal was rejected.

The young prince, greatly upset over this rebuff, asked his mother, Queen Mary, for her advice. The queen listened sympathetically to her son's tale of woe. Then she told him she wanted to ask just one question before advising him. Did he really love Elizabeth only? would he be able to find a substitute if Elizabeth proved reluctant? After a moment's consideration, he replied that he would marry Elizabeth or no one else. "Well, then," said his mother, "there is only one way open to you. Go and ask her again."

So the young prince put his pride in his pocket, gathered up his remaining courage, and arranged another interview with Elizabeth. He probably stuttered as he repeated his proposal, remembering what had happened to him the first time at her hands. She refused him again.

Not knowing what to do then, he returned to his mother, Queen Mary, for advice. Again she listened quietly—some say, severely—to the whole story. She showed him every sympathy and, after hearing all he had to say, indicated that she had one question to ask before she could advise him. The question was: "Do you really want her after this rebuff? There are plenty of other young ladies around who would be delighted to have a prince as a husband. I myself could show you some." But poor

George was quite clear about his feelings. It was Elizabeth or no one at all. "Then," said his mother, "in that case there is only one way open to you. Go and ask her again."

So, after a considerable period of mental preparation, the young prince approached the pretty young Scottish lady the third time. In the meantime, she had noticed how serious the prince was. His love and determination to win her had indeed been constant. She saw that the great effort he made in coming the third time, putting his pride in his pocket, demonstrated his singleness of purpose. And she began to recognize something new in herself. His undoubted love toward her was beginning to kindle an answering fire in her own heart. His warmth of love, even though he was awkward and not very good at courting a young lady's affection, was beginning to warm her affection toward him. In short, his love began to kindle her love, and she began to transmit some of the love which she received from him. She began to feel she was able to say that she loved and admired him in his singleness of purpose and constancy. Thus, the story goes, began one of the really happy families in the annals of royal households. And this love lasted until the king's death.

Love begets love. But it often has to be very patient, long-suffering and kind until the fire is kindled in the prospective partner's heart. The Scriptures say that *God woos in one way or another every man and woman ever born.*[7] Through the circumstances of life, or through the Scriptures, he quietly goes on as the years pass, until we begin to return to him some of the warmth of love which he has for us. For we are told that God has his delight among the sons of men.[8] He *loves* us,[9] rejectors though we have been of his overtures toward us. He is working toward the day when we may begin to return to him the same love, and to delight in his friendship as he will delight in ours.

Once kindled, this love must be regularly tended in order to maintain the warmth of the blaze which God intends our love to be—warming and refreshing to both partners, so that both can rejoice in the happiness which love brings. God is love and we were so constructed in his image that we can only flourish when bathed in such love—breathing it in and giving it out.

But, it would be one-sided to leave the story here. All love stories do not end this way. We must look at one other less pleasant possibility.

THE FINAL REFUSAL

There comes a time in every love affair when a *final* answer toward the wooer must be made. This *final* answer may be either yes or no. One day the wooed one may make a rejection which, although she perhaps did not know it, was the final one. It turns out to be permanent. In the one case she may, of course, die. That finishes the wooing of a mortal man—when immortality lays hold of the prospective bride.

Another possibility is that the wooer may cease to woo. The "wooed" is not the only one who has a free will to accept or reject the wooer. *God as the wooer has a free will too*—to stop or to continue wooing according to his infinite wisdom. He can decide how long to woo and be rejected and also when to stop wooing altogether. Even this final decision to stop wooing will, we are told, be made on the basis of love. It will, accordingly, be put off as long as at all possible.

There is a third and last possibility. If *the wooed marries another,* then further courtship by the first suitor would be thoroughly out of order and *outside the confines of love.* The Scriptures say quite clearly that this state of affairs may be reached in the spiritual sense. There comes a time when a man "marries this world," and after that, God no longer offers his salvation, his "marriage relationship" to him. His Spirit strives with him no longer. A man's spirit and God's Spirit become forever estranged, for man's spirit finally "marries another," selling itself to this world and its rebellion against the Most High. A man can close his ears finally to the "still small voice"

that so long had whispered to him to return—he then "marries another" and the pleading rightly stops forever.

We humans can seldom clearly see when such a final act takes place. We cannot determine when God's Spirit gives a man up forever. But that such does occur is perfectly clear, even though it is invisible to man's mortal eye. As Wesley's beautiful hymn put it, Jesus is the lover of man's soul. He is the patient lover. But there comes a time when all courtship ceases and when a man can irrevocably "marry another" and cut off God's striving permanently. This can be done in many ways. We can give ourselves entirely over to material things such as a career, money, or social standing. It may be the love of things more definitely sinful that cuts us off. In extreme cases we can "sell ourselves to the devil" quite consciously—as many Nazis did when they knowingly cooperated with Hitler in liquidating human beings in the interests of their own promotion within the party. Many do the same just as effectively when they value promotion in their jobs before promotion in the kingdom of heaven. They do not seek "the kingdom of heaven *first*."[10] Some men resolve never to discuss spiritual matters again because "they disturb." For them, the courtship is over; they're married to another.

The New Testament letter to the Hebrews speaks of that cessation. "Today, when you hear his voice, do not harden your hearts as in the rebellion, on the day of testing in the wilderness, where your fathers put me to the test and saw my works for forty years. Therefore I was provoked with that generation, and said, 'They always go astray in their hearts; they have not known my ways.' As I swore in my wrath, '*They shall never enter my rest.*'"[11]

The context of this statement shows that the Lord spoke and spoke again, and wooed and wooed again, but the Hebrews of that generation closed their hearts and inward ears. In the end God gave them up, and that generation, except for Joshua and Caleb, never entered the promised land but perished in the wilderness. This serves as a parable for us, to whom God also speaks. We can be so occupied with the trials and joys of this life that we, too, do not hear. We, too, can miss the joy and rest of his love by acting as did the Hebrews.

"For it is *impossible to restore again to repentance* those who have once been enlightened, who have tasted the heavenly gift, and have become partakers of the Holy Spirit, and have tasted the goodness of the word of God and the powers of the age to come, *if they then commit apostasy,* since they crucify the Son of God on their own account and hold him up to contempt."[12]

This warning is to those who have at one time responded to God's wooing, and have therefore tasted his goodness, and then cease to respond. A time comes when it is impossible to renew them, for the striving of God's Spirit with them ceases.

Another Scripture passage speaks in exactly the same tenor: "For if we sin deliberately after receiving the knowledge of the truth, there no longer remains a sacrifice for sins, but a fearful prospect of judgment, and a fury of fire which will consume the adversaries. . . . How much worse punishment do you think will be deserved by the man who has spurned the Son of God, and profaned the blood of the covenant by which he was sanctified, and *outraged the Spirit of grace*? . . . It is a fearful thing to fall into the hands of the living God."[13]

I take this warning for myself, believing that I can learn from all of Scripture. The point is, God can and does speak to men; he does woo. If they respond he allows them to taste in this life the things of his kingdom of love. But his wooing is *dynamic,* and it is dependent on our daily response. Continual spurning may end in our "marrying another forever." Then his wooing stops, for we have committed the sin of spurning the Son of God. Rejecting God's grace in Christ simply means declaring ourselves as candidates for no grace, which is the same thing as being ripe for judgment.

This raises the whole question of judgment at the hands of a so-called loving and gracious God. Can we accept this? Is all suffering a judgment? Or must suffering and judgment be kept apart in our minds? Suffering certainly accompanies judgment, but is all suffering judgment?

6

Suffering and Anguish—
Any Reasonable Interpretation?

RESENTMENT AGAINST PURPOSELESS SUFFERING

Many people as they undergo suffering resent what is happening because they can often see no constructive purpose behind it. Is it cosmic sadism? When we *can* see a good reason for pain or suffering, as in surgery or the dentist's drill, we can endure it without resentment, even though the actual pain may be worse. The relief of knowing *why* is tremendous and can change resentment and impatience into anticipation and patience.

"Senseless" suffering, such as we see when innocent children are destroyed or mutilated in war, sickness, plague or famine, makes our anger and impatience rise. The impatience increases when we see pain which is not only "senseless" or "random" but apparently designed and calculated, or even "refined," as is the pain at the root of malaria, for surely that pain looks directly sadistic in its very mechanism, as we have already mentioned. When senseless pain is apparently not merely adventitious, but designed, the average honest-thinking person tends to lose restraint in considering it.

A good example of this arises in considering, as did C. S. Lewis, the deafness of a musical genius such as Beethoven.[1] An absolute master of the art and science of sound struck down with stone deafness! Could a greater refinement of apparent sadism be conceived? Hence the impatience of many when they merely begin to consider the problem of suffering.

Yet, on the other hand, anyone who considers himself to be a Christian is warned on every side to expect both joy and suffering as normally as summer and winter. Both are, according to Scripture, integral parts of the Christian experience. Just because he is a Christian he is not excused from suffering with the rest of mankind. Rather, he is promised additional suffering just because he is a Christian. The apostle Paul says explicitly that the Christian must enter the kingdom not only in joy but also through the gates of many trials, tribulations and sufferings, being forsaken of man, and apparently by God too, before reaching the final gate of death.[2]

Why? If we could only get a reasonable answer, our misery could be borne with more patience and less rebellion. Surely a good, loving, omnipotent and kind God could have found some method of reducing the sharpness of the dreadful realities of living and dying. Can he be both good and just while quietly sitting by and letting the slaughter and anguish go on and on, generation after generation?

IF GOD IS GOOD, WILL HE HURT US?

Lewis puts this very question in another light when he writes, "If God's goodness is inconsistent with his hurting us, then either God is not good or there is no God; for, in the only life we know he hurts us beyond our worst fears and beyond all we can imagine."[3] Plainly, this means that if we believe in God at all, we must believe that it *is* consistent with his perfect nature, kindness and love to hurt us and to leave us wallowing in our own blood, as it were, right up to the end.

Lewis adds a rider to his statement which asks, in effect: If we accept that in this life God can hurt us beyond all that we can imagine, and that this hurting is consistent with his goodness, have we any valid reasons for believing that he should not, if necessary, continue hurting us in the same way after this mortal life is over?[4] Obviously there is no *moral* reason why he should not, if spirits can endure suffering as mortal men do. Numerous passages of Scripture need to be examined carefully in this connection. Neither Lewis nor we are suggesting that the torments of hell are universal after death! The real question is whether suffering serves any purpose in this life and in that to come.

We can, however, go one step further and still remain on safe ground. If God has reasons—other than sadism, which we cannot attribute to thim—for hurting us now in this mortal life, he might, conceivably, have equally good reasons for continuing the same process afterward, in death. Clarity on such questions will only come by first asking ourselves, "What does the Scripture say?" And second, from our answer to why he hurts us now and what he intends to achieve by it in this life and beyond.

WAS CHRIST EVER IN MAN'S POSITION?

It is often helpful in dealing with such questions to find out whether Christ the Man was ever in the same position as we in regard to suffering. If he was (and in other matters he plainly was, except in questions of sin), then the investigation of what suffering achieved in him will, perhaps, provide the answer as to what it is supposed to achieve in us.

Accordingly, looking at one of the most obvious cases of Christ's suffering—the cross—may help to solve the problem. God the Father "stood passively by," as it were, while men crucified his own beloved Son. There can be no doubt about the fact that Christ was the Son of his love, the second Person of the Trinity in whom he was well pleased. The Son loved the

Father and the Father loved the Son, for the disciples and others heard the voice from heaven saying so. Yet, it is also a fact that God remained "passive" while the awful deed was done, just as he remained "passive" while millions of Jews, his own people, were gassed in brutal cynicism.

To make matters worse, the Scripture says this brutal act was the culmination of the prophecy that Christ was the *Lamb of God slain from the foundation of the world.* Thus, the cruel cross was an eternally foreseen event—an event which God presided at eternally in a purely passive manner in that he did not stop it. Therefore, the hurting of the beloved one must have been consistent with God's eternal character. In fact, God himself suffered, for he was in Christ as he suffered (2 Cor. 5:19), so he was not really passive, for he actively suffered— and suffers—too.

THE CROSS AND GOD'S LOVE

This means that if the central doctrine of the Christian faith, the cross, is true, then it is obviously also true that it must be consistent with God's eternal love to hurt those he loves best —including himself—even to the point of what we would call barbarism, for the cross is barbaric. Considering the barbarism of the cross, which God eternally allowed, one is tempted with Lewis to say: "God forgive God."[5]

The conclusion we must draw, then, from the fact that Christ did suffer the cross is that God allowed Christ, his beloved one, to be "put under the harrow" (to use Lewis' terms) from which there was no escape, even to death. In fact, God was in Christ as he allowed this act. The same applies to the whole human race and to biology, which can also be said to be "under the harrow" in a large way.

Whichever way we look we find the same picture in principle. Christ on the eternal cruel cross and a so-called God of love behind him and, indeed, in him. Humanity and biology for millennia "under the harrow" too, and yet, allegedly, according to the Scripture, a God of love behind us, who is until now entirely passive at the spectacle. Confronted with this situation, what Lewis feared was not so much a loss of belief in any God at all with its concomitant victory of pure materialism in him. That solution would have been too easy, for it would have meant that a simple overdose of sleeping pills at any time could have gotten him out from "under the harrow" forever. Far too simple! What worried Lewis was that the "harrow" might mean that man and biology were all trapped, as it were, in a laboratory in which God might be the eternal vivisector and we the rats![6] Lewis says that the despair in which the Son of God died when he cried out, "My God, why hast thou forsaken me?"[7] might have been the result of Christ finding out that the cross was, in reality, a carefully baited laboratory trap which sprang at death and from which there was no escape after God had lured him into it.

Looked at dispassionately, surely even an admittedly fallen person like myself, possessing scarcely a trace of the love I attribute to a God of love, could not have stood passively by while they crucified him—or gassed the millions of Jews with prussic acid. Even a person like myself, who is no example of love in any sense, would have tried to arrange things better than that and would not have allowed my dearest to be treated thus, right to the bitter end! But, then, if we take that view, God must be morally inferior—even to me—which is completely nihilistic. We shall have to scrap that view too, for it leads straight to the destruction of all rational thought on the subject.

Of course God is more compassionate than I. But why then was he so relentlessly passive at the cross? Why doesn't he relent at all the millennia of human and biological agony? At the slow starvation of millions? At the sight of the cancer victims, dying while they yet live? At the sight of children and old people losing eyes or limbs at play or on the street? If all this monstrous situation is allowed by a God who is good, and therefore not sadistic, what is all the grief and anguish about?

HURTING IN ORDER TO HEAL

Can the key to the sore problem be found in the following considerations: Can we allow that to do good there may be occasions when we must apparently do that which looks as though it were bad? Put another way, can we hurt to heal? Obviously we can allow that, for every good surgeon and dentist does so regularly and routinely, nobody even raising an eyebrow about it, for it is so obvious. To be a really good surgeon or dentist one has to be perfectly relentless quite regularly in hurting in order to do good. If, every time I flinched, gripped the dentist's chair, or drew back my head in pain at the relentless drill, he were to stop and consider ending the torture and filling up the still dirty cavity with amalgam, he would be less than a good dentist. He would not be being good, or even kind or loving to his patient if he were anything but absolutely unrelenting in his thoroughness in inflicting this therapeutic suffering. We would all be in trouble again in no time if he did relent. And then all the pain he had already inflicted in the early drillings would have been in vain. Thus, to be good he has to be absolutely relentless in his infliction of suffering. He has to be apparently passive to the pain he is causing. Not only does he not stop the pain but he goes on inflicting more distress on me. Does he seem devoid of feeling? In reality, of course, his passiveness to suffering, his apparent lack of feeling and his relentlessness are merely motivated by common sense and consideration for his patient, even though the intolerable pain might persuade me otherwise.

For anyone who has undergone root treatment of a molar tooth, two further points will emerge to throw light on this problem. The bacterial infection not only causes excruciating pain, but the toxins released into the blood will poison the patient to such an extent that his very consciousness may become clouded. He may scarcely know what he is doing because of the pain and poison. Then the dentist begins work with his awful drill. The pain becomes more excruciating until the center of the infection is reached. Then the poison pressure is released, and immediate relief is felt, though it is not yet complete. As soon as no more poison is being released into the blood, the head begins to clear and the pain to subside.

First, then, in order to remove the hurt of decay, sometimes more pain has to be inflicted—worse than that of the original sickness. But the worse pain acts curatively on the first pain and purges it away. Second, only when the basic trouble begins to be cured does clarity of thought return.

THE SCRIPTURAL POSITION

Scripture teaches, in essence, precisely this view on the meaning of suffering. The fall introduced the "decay" of humanity and nature which results in the hurt which afflicts us. Thus arose the pain of the festering tooth pulp. To cure this festering mess, the Bible says a good but relentless surgeon is needed to drill and drill until reality is too horrible to bear, until flesh and blood can no longer take it—until we believe we're forsaken by God and man. The Bible describes in detail both the setting in of the decay and its radical if painful cure. Our species has decayed from its original state and become, as it were, a lower or decayed species, as I have described elsewhere.[8] To cure this decay and loss of species requires radical and drastic treatment involving, first of all, the reaching of the "focal point of infection," and then the "removal of the deformities produced by the decay." Christ's death and resurrection "reached the focal point" of the trouble, as it were. But the "deformities of the decay" have also to be corrected, and that takes time and can be expected to be painful.

One of these "deformities" is connected with the "clouding of the intellectual and rational process" which accompanies the fall. The apostle Paul described them in Romans 1 as a "darkening of the mind" so that the normal, logical thought processes for which we were designed became garbled. One of the by-products of suffering is seen here. For although suffering and toxins may "knock us silly," the removal of the latter can bring clarity of thought. It is a fact that sin darkens the mind. The corollary that redemption and holiness enlighten the mind is also true. For salvation not only redeems us from a lost eternity; it also redeems us from a lost, clouded, befuddled life at present. It makes the face and intellect radiant and removes the darkness, even intellectually speaking. By taking away our sin, we become saved for eternity. But we must not forget that this same saving process brings light and radiance to the heart and intellect right now, the process being one of growth—growth in this life.

ACCURATE SURGERY OR WHOLESALE BUTCHERY?

Can the skilled, accurately aimed work of the dentist on a tooth, with its concomitant pain and healing, be compared with the wild, undisciplined, purely destructive agony which afflicts much of mankind today? Can we believe that war, the wholesale gassing of the innocent, and the mutilation of children and the aged are the work of a "surgeon" in curing mankind? Here again, for any satisfactory answer, we must turn back to the archetype of all barbarous suffering, namely, the cruel cross.

Is it possible to believe that when wicked men, inspired by hatred and jealousy, decided to take Jesus, hold a mock trial, scourge him with their equivalent of a cat-o'-nine-tails, display him all night for the raucous amusement of the troops, and then finally drive iron stakes through his hands and feet, raising him on a cross to bleed to death by exhaustion—can we reasonably hold that such a performance was the work of a skilled surgeon in his efforts to cure the world of its disease?

THE EXACT THERAPY OF THE CROSS

The Christian position is frankly that this was the case: that

God, with the butchery of the cross, did cure the world of its disease, and that the cross was the work of a skilled surgeon, even though it looked from the human point of view like the exclusively destructive and adventitious work of the ribald Roman soldiers and hateful Pharisees. It looks so very much like this that the cross was considered by the Greeks to be so unworthy of divinity that it was a sheer "scandal." But the fact is, outward appearances may deceive. They certainly did in the case of the Son of God dying the death of a common criminal. May not outward appearances deceive also in our particular cases of suffering?

The reason for this deception is simple. Outwardly wicked men cruelly put him to death and that was all that man ever saw of the process. But behind the scenes the great surgeon did an unseen work through Christ's suffering. Unseen by men, Christ took into his own body the very "virus" which was at the root of man's sickness—the turning of man's back upon the only good one and his perfect will. The Bible says that this turning is "sin." It is as though Christ in his death took the organism of decay (sin) away from me, as well as the *products of decay* (the egoism, hate, impatience, untruthfulness, etc., which result from and are produced by a sinful attitude), which are the toxins (sins), and allowed the organism to be cultured in his body until it killed him. A parasite may kill the host organism, as when the influenza virus kills the man it lives on as a parasite. But in killing the host it also kills itself at the same time. So Christ took on both the *causative organism* (sin) together with its "toxins" (sins), such as my hates, lies and general unrighteousness, so that mankind and I could be freed from both by embracing his act. In taking into his body the lethal organism, as well as the products of its activities (metabolism, if one will), he himself had to die. But, in that the "parasite" (sin) killed the "host organism," the parasite killed itself too.

This was the secret surgery or therapy which went on unseen to the human eye when they crucufied him. Thus, the senselessness of the cross is only superficial—superficial to the uninitiated. Its senselessness becomes sense to those who probe to the bottom of the mystery and find that he did, in fact, bear their sin and sins in his own body on the tree. This fact accounts for the reality of their experience at the beginnings of the secret but healing therapy wrought for them at Calvary.

The actual mechanism of this secret therapy is quite simple. The "virus" which schemed and killed the human race and brought the fall to our universe was known as disobedience to the known good will of God. That is, it was a turning away from the only good, which automatically brought with it an embracing of the bad. The organism which introduced death to man and biology was characterized by turning away from the sustainer and Creator of life itself.

Christ at Calvary simply reversed this process of rejecting God's known will by turning to, embracing and doing God's known will, even though it meant his own suffering and death. Man's act in turning away from God was reversed by Christ when he embraced God for us anew with his will. However, he embraced not only the basic cause of the ill—the turning away —but he took on himself the consequences, the "metabolic products," as it were, of that fatal wrong choice. He took my sickness and my sicknesses on himself. No one watching at the cross actually saw him do this. No one knows just how he did it, that is, just what mechanism he used. All we know is that we could not do it, for none of us could die in a valid way before God for the sin of another. All we know is that the Father gave his permission and command to Christ to lay down his life as a ransom for many. And Christ obediently did just that. The man Christ reversed man's disobedience.

A LESS UGLY WAY?

This is, I suppose, the legal way of looking at the therapy

Christ accomplished for me at the cross. As such, it is of vast importance, providing, as it does, the basis of salvation from the guilt of sin for eternity. Some will say it is horrible. It is. To think that God could find no other method than a bloody cross, cruel iron nails through hands and feet, before he could redeem me from Adam's fatal mistake, fills me with dismay. Surely a more genteel, aesthetically acceptable method could have been found for such a momentous piece of therapy.

This brings us to the second point we must make on this subject. It concerns the blood, the sweat, and the forsakenness of the cross of Calvary, in short, the ugliness and horror of such a piece of restorative therapy. For the utter cruelty of it shocks even wicked men. Let us look then at this second great problem of the cross—its ugliness.

It is written of Christ: "In the days of his flesh, Jesus offered up prayers and supplications, with loud cries and tears, to him who was able to save him from death, and he was heard for his godly fear. *Although he was a Son, he learned obedience through what he suffered;* and being made perfect he became the source of eternal salvation to all who obey him."[9]

That is an almost incredible statement for the writer of the letter to the Hebrews to have made. The Son of God had always been perfect from eternity until he came into time at the incarnation. And during the incarnation he was without sin, and therefore, still perfect. What the writer is teaching here will answer our question as to why God chose such a cruel, ugly and bloody method of redemptive therapy.

MADE PERFECT

The process of "being made perfect" referred to here means, in this context, being "made mature." If a child is perfect in mind and body, there is nothing we can complain about. But his perfection as a child needs to grow into the mature perfection of an adult. This process is one of growth in body, mind and experience. There is no quick way around it. To be genuine, it must be gone through experimentally.

This is exactly what Christ went through experimentally as a man. He was perfect from a child onward. But the Bible says he grew in wisdom and stature—that is, he *matured* by his experience as a man. Even though he was the second Person of the Trinity, he was perfected by growing up as a man, for he gathered actual experience of manhood which he lacked experimentally before the incarnation. He certainly *knew* all about manhood before he became a man, because he was omniscient. But now he experienced manhood in the body—and matured or became experienced, and therefore perfected, in it.

Now notice what some of this manhood experience involved for Christ—something he, as God, had not *experienced as a man* before: "In the days of his flesh, Jesus offered up prayers and supplications, with loud cries and tears, to him who was able to save him from death." God the Son had never had *that* experience, common to all men, while he was God the Son and had never yet experienced the incarnation. It was the fight between the will to be obedient and the terrible reality of a bloody death on the tree. This was a new experience. Here we have anxiety, anguish and suffering—right up to bloody sweat—in anticipation of the abyss of such a death. He matured as a man by the experience of anguished prayer in faith to him who could deliver him. We are assured that he was heard because of his godly fear. But he was only saved *from* death by going down *through* death and thus being led out of it after tasting it.

The result, then, of this seemingly unreasonable and cruel death of the cross and the anguish which preceded it was that although he was a Son, *yet he learned obedience through what he suffered.* Of course, he had always been obedient to the Father's will—the two wills were always congruent and the Father loved the Son and the Son the Father. But here was a new experience for God the Son, the experiencing of the anguish of facing death such as all creatures, but not God, face. The God of life was to die for all his creatures and share all their ugly experiences.

The anguish and suffering of the cross and the preceding events demonstrated that Christ was perfectly obedient to the Father in all things. The experience of the unnameable pain, anguish and forsakenness of the cross did something to the incarnate Son of God which would have been impossible before the incarnation. The discipline, the setting of his face as a flint to go to Jerusalem to face it all, the refusal of even the analgesic (the myrrh) before the nails were driven through him, all that *perfected even him, the Son of God—as Man.* Thus, the fact of the cross laid down the legal basis for our salvation, but the *bloody cross* showed what suffering and anguish can do if accepted as Jesus accepted them. His death was expiatory for sin. But the *manner* of his death served at the same time as a teacher of obedience to God the Man; it was a maturer, a perfecter of the perfect one. If the Son of God as man was matured in his experience and learned obedience by it, then we find yet another secret, hidden element in the mode of "therapy" God introduced by his Son to cure the creation of its fatal malady.

It will be obvious then, that, purely legally, Christ's bare death—by any method—would have secured our salvation for eternity. However, it was, perhaps, not immediately obvious why such a shocking and barbarous route to death needed to be taken—a route which made the cross a scandal to the Greeks and a stumbling block to the Jews. No wonder so few of the Greeks or Jews could understand it without the extra information given on the subject of suffering by the New Testament—and by experience too.

SUFFERING—NOT SENSELESS

Thus, the anguish and suffering of the cross are not senseless. They are a refined even though drastic therapy, hidden to the eyes of the mortal man in general. But their function teaches us why the whole Bible is full of references to pain, suffering and anguish. Every person who embraces the death of Christ (and his resurrection) as his basis for eternal salvation is warned to expect, as a matter of routine, sufferings of some sort. Christ having suffered in the flesh, he is told, is warning enough for us to arm ourselves with the same mind—that is, to be on the lookout for the squalls of suffering which certainly await the consistent Christian.[10] In giving us salvation, Christ suffered. In accepting that salvation, suffering will certainly find us out.

Further, we are told that the disciple is not above his Master even in these matters.[11] *This means that, in this context, if the perfection or maturation of the Master could not be effected without the anguish of suffering, neither can the maturation or perfection of the disciple be accomplished by any other means.* The Christian who thinks he can get through the Christian life without this sort of perfecting is living in a fool's paradise. The disciple is *not* above his Master even in learning matters.

The New Testament is full of teaching of this kind, teaching which is seldom even touched upon today, for by its very nature it is unpopular to the natural human. Paul the apostle, when writing to the Philippians, informed them that "it has been *granted* to you that for the sake of Christ you should not only *believe* in him but also *suffer* for his sake."[12] Surely it would have been unnecessary for Paul to have told the Philippians that *it had been granted* them not only to believe but also to suffer if just believing without suffering was an ideal state. Clearly, no one wants suffering. But, in the light of the above, it must be a special privilege. Christ did not relish it. He sweat blood in anticipation of it. But he endured it as a privilege in view of the glory of the maturity gained by it.

This means, again, that even for us mortals "senseless" suffering need not be pointless. It may be more than the mere adventitious agony produced in a mortal body of flesh and blood. It can be the gateway to special results in our characters. In any case, it is poor policy to avoid suffering by disobedience, for Christ embraced trials and suffered because of obedience, thus being matured and perfected thereby. It is the Christian path to try to follow the same policy. For by following this policy Christ has been matured and exalted by the Father to his right hand. He has committed the entire government of the world into Christ's capable hands—hands rendered capable, mature and fit for the job by being obedient even to letting them be pierced at the cross.

Is it because the fruit of suffering is so little known in the Western churches that we have so few "giants" in the land today? In the East, behind the Iron and Bamboo curtains, the total number of Christians has been reduced greatly by suffering. But the proportion of "giants," mature Christians, has certainly greatly increased there.

PROMISED TRIBULATION

The Bible—both the Old and the New Testaments—is crammed with references to suffering, anguish, tribulation, grief, trial and affliction.[13] For example, there is this rather neglected text by the apostle Paul: "But whatever gain I had, I counted as loss for the sake of Christ. Indeed, I count everything as loss because of the surpassing worth of knowing Christ Jesus my Lord. For his sake I have suffered the loss of all things, and count them as refuse, in order that I may gain Christ and be found in him, not having a righteousness of my own, based on law, but that which is through faith in Christ . . . that I may know him and the power of his resurrection, *and may share his sufferings, becoming like him in his death, that if possible I may attain the resurrection [out] from [among] the dead.*"[14]

THE REASON WHY

It is clear from the letter to the Romans that Paul knew and experienced salvation on the basis of a *gift of God* and not on the basis of any works he had done. Nothing he could do could save him from the penalty of sin. On the Damascus road he had learned that his own works could not help him but that Christ's work could and did. Why, then, does Paul now insist so much on the value of the *work* of suffering he had done in losing everything for Christ's sake? Those losses would never *save* him.

As we read the cited passage carefully it becomes obvious that Paul is referring to the *value of sufferings and losses in gaining a knowledge of the surpassing worth of knowing Christ.* He is referring to a process which can only be described as one of Christian maturity or perfection. He suffered the loss of every privilege which he had possessed as a well-respected Pharisee in order to be obedient to Christ. No doubt this caused anguish. But his losses were not only abstract. He was whipped, imprisoned, mishandled, shipwrecked and generally treated as the offscouring of the world for Christ's sake. He couples these experiences with the *greater experience which resulted directly from their knowing the surpassing worth of Christ.* Most of us Western Christians know little of this. Is it because we have not sought out the only maturing process known in Scripture leading to this knowledge—and to Christ? Paul's obedience, like Christ's obedience, in suffering while doing the will and Word of God is the key to such depth of experience.

But more about the maturing process is to be discovered in Philippians 3. *Christ was exalted to power because he was fitted for it by the things he obediently suffered.* Paul says in effect precisely the same of himself and his own exaltation. For he couples *his loss and his suffering with a capacity to take part in what he calls the "out-resurrection"* (exanastasis) which he regarded not as a matter of course for every Christian but as that which depends on Christian maturity. We all know—as do the Muslims—that all of us, small and great, wicked and good, rich and poor, will be resurrected at the great day of final judgment to receive the things done in our bodies. But before the day of general "anastasis" there will be an "exanastasis" of rising of the dead, not in a general, but in a special, resurrection. This will be at the time of the return of our Lord in glory to set up his kingdom on earth and reign. In order to rule and reign, Christ is looking for men and women *among his redeemed* who have allowed themselves to be matured for this high office—*by means of the same process by which he was made fit for it—by anguish and suffering.*

Apparently Paul's aim was to obediently accept the same type of loss and suffering that his Master had gone through in order to become prepared for high office with Christ. All this is *based* upon the free gift of salvation by the blood of Christ. But in building upon this sure basis of free salvation, a maturing or a perfection process occurs by means of suffering in the will of God, foreseen both by Christ and by Paul. Paul's attitude of heart is confirmed by his instruction to Timothy: "If we have *died* with him, we shall also *live* with him; *if we endure,* we shall also *reign* with him; if we deny him, he also will deny us."[15] This surely clinches the matter. The Christian owes his *redemption* to the *free gift of God.* But he owes his *degree of exaltation* to close knowledge of the surpassing worth of Christ and close association with him and his purposes in his kingdom, and to the maturation processes which fitted even the Son for his supreme office in the kingdom. *The experiences of suffering, endurance and anguish in obedience to the will of God, no matter how outwardly senseless and adventitious they may appear, are the therapeutic instruments God used on his Son and uses on all his redeemed who declare themselves willing for the process.*

The same process produces not only the surpassing knowledge of his will, but it also makes us useful to others. "For *because he himself has suffered and been tempted, he is able to help those who are tempted.*"[16] On this basis, who could be better fitted to help mankind than the Son of Man who has been through the same kind of temptation—though far more acute? This establishes a bond of confidence between us and him. He understands because he has experienced the fire of anguish. Therefore he can help us because his is a sympathy engendered by understanding. Our lot and his as mortals were once congruous. It gives me confidence toward him. If I suffer I can help those who are suffering, even as Christ has helped me.

PERFECTION

This leads us to the third point. The first point was that Christ died and rose again to justify and redeem us, giving us the basis for fellowship with a holy God. The second point was that his sufferings and endurance were the means of qualification and maturation for his exaltation to the right hand of God the Father. In a parallel manner, the sufferings of Christians (for the gospel's sake and in general) are calculated to mature them for high office with him in his kingdom. The third point is also directly concerned with suffering and its consequences. Peter develops the subject in saying, "Since therefore *Christ suffered in the flesh, arm yourselves with the same thought [mind or will], for whoever has suffered in the flesh has ceased from sin, so as to live for the rest of the time in the flesh no longer by human passions but by the will of God.*"[17]

Peter was referring to "suffering in the flesh" which, he says, leads to ceasing from sin in the flesh. But the same principle also applies to matters not necessarily directly connected with the flesh, as he also confirms: "For one is approved if, mindful of God, he endures pain while suffering unjustly."[18] This simply means that any discomfort we have to endure because of our faithfulness to God's will eventually leads to our being "approved." In fact, Peter says that as Christ suffered the same kind of discomfort for our sakes, so he left us "an example, that you should follow in his steps."[19] This, then, is the line of action to which we "have been called."

Therefore, according to Peter, suffering leads to ceasing from sin, and approval before God. Is it then any wonder that, after his death and resurrection, Christ asked the disciples questions which bring the whole problem of suffering into focus: "Was it not necessary that the Christ *should suffer these things* and enter into his glory?"[20] "The Christ *should suffer* and on the third day rise from the dead."[21] The same subject was the theme of Paul's three-week argument with the Jews in Thessalonica: "And Paul went in, as was his custom, and *for three weeks he argued with them from the Scriptures, explaining and proving that it was necessary for the Christ to suffer and to rise from the dead.*"[22] Among other things, suffering made Christ "approved."

It is generally conceded that Christ's *death* is basic to the Christian's salvation. But the *suffering type of death* is not usually emphasized. Perhaps it is too barbaric for our cultured society to bear. Regardless of our reactions to the awfulness of the death on the cross, *God chose it* in order to bring to mankind *a full salvation*—not only from the *guilt* of sin but also from its *power*, not only to save us from eternal damnation but also to demonstrate to us how to become approved in the same way that Christ became approved. In fact, it was to teach us how to cease from sin.

REJOICING IN SUFFERING

Paul sums it all up: "So we do not lose heart. Though our outer nature is wasting away, our inner nature is being renewed every day. *For this slight momentary affliction is preparing for us an eternal weight of glory beyond all comparison.*"[23] Clearly, Christ's death and resurrection are the cornerstones of any salvation that will take us to heaven. But Paul is talking about something built as a superstructure on the foundation of salvation. *It is an eternal, incomparable weight of glory founded upon salvation, God's free gift.* And it is our temporary afflictions, the suffering and pain borne in the will of God, which make us approved for incomparable glory, just as afflictions and sufferings brought approval to Christ after he had patiently and triumphantly borne them. Temporary afflictions exchanged for an incomparable weight of glory! Paul considered it a bargain. So he acted on it immediately!

A POSSIBLE MISUNDERSTANDING

Of course, one might say that if suffering and afflictions are so useful and well rewarded in the will of God, then let us afflict and scourge our fellowmen all we can and seek suffering ourselves. We are doing them a favor by hurting them or ourselves. This seems to echo the old argument: Let us sin willfully so that grace may abound. Let us seek and provoke suffering! God forbid! The dentist does not willfully or wantonly bore holes anywhere and everywhere in our teeth to stop the future possibility of decay. God is the surgeon, so let him operate just where he finds it necessary. He may and will use wicked men as his scalpel. He has promised to reward them for their evil intentions because they afflict others just for the sake of hurting and killing. Though he uses that same evil for his own purposes, that doesn't give us the right to sin so that grace may abound by hurting others or ourselves unnecessarily.

To indiscriminately inflict pain is wanton. Jesus himself never regarded pain and suffering as good things in themselves, for he abolished them by healing on many occasions. He also told us to do the same. The Scripture speaks of death itself as the last *enemy*. Pain falls into the same category. Pain and death entered into the world by the fall, when man turned his back upon God. The point is that God reverses the evils of pain and death to produce a glorious result—to glorify his Son and to glorify man when they both withstand and endure pain and death in doing his will. This is how God triumphs over evil—not by "stopping" it, but by using it to his greater glory.

In another book I have attempted to describe the character

of the Man Jesus and have used the Sermon on the Mount to illustrate some of my points.[24] He said of himself that he was "meek" and "humble" of spirit. Such an attitude of mind would scarcely be compatible with his having created the world by the principles of chance and natural selection of the stronger specimens as laid down by Darwin. For Jesus did not destroy the sick, the weak nor the importunate beggars, unfitted for the commercial life of his day, as Darwin's principles would demand.

GENTLING PROCESS

A minister wrote to me, after reading the book cited, about the subject of the meekness of Jesus, pointing out that the word *meek* is often misunderstood. In the context used in the Sermon on the Mount the word translated by *meek* really means "gentled" or "broken in" as those terms are applied to horses trained to work in harness. The minister recounted how, as a boy, he had worked on a farm and helped with "gentling" horses, breaking them in for farm work. Later the horses were often used for pulling out tree stumps prior to preparing wasteland for arable purposes.

The untrained wild horses were useless for doing the skilled work necessary for removing tree stumps. They had to be thoroughly "tamed" before they could work constructively with other horses in teams. The taming or breaking-in and "gentling" process was a prior necessity for useful work. Once they had been submitted to the sometimes harsh process of breaking in, which involved whipping and punishment as well as rewards, they worked productively the rest of their lives and obviously enjoyed it thoroughly. As their experience grew, the reins could be left on their necks and they would go by themselves from tree stump to tree stump, assume the correct position, wait for the chains to be hitched to the trunk, and then with all their strength—nipping and nudging one another in the process—pull out the stump. If a stump did not come up at the first pull they would move to a more favorable angle and try again.

Affliction and suffering can work as a "gentling" process, fitting us for God's work in the present world and the next. This is the true meaning of the word *meek* as Jesus used it. What if the abysmal suffering of mankind and of nature, a result of the fall into sin, is now being used in God's good hands to "gentle" us all—even as it "gentled" his Son? The stakes are indeed high. Suffering makes us kind to others who suffer. But what if a bloody war, a rule of tyranny (while being recognized as culpable sin on the part of their perpetrators, who are promised a just reward for their deeds) is really working out an incomparable weight of glory for all those who allow themselves to be "gentled" and disciplined thereby? If this is so, it would be a fatal blow to the despair and nihilism into which our generation is so obviously falling. If eternal glory were to result (and the Bible says it will), then we could, with the Christians of old, rejoice in suffering and jubilate with the apostle Paul: *"We rejoice in our sufferings, knowing that suffering produces endurance, and endurance produces character, and character produces hope, and hope does not disappoint us, because God's love has been poured into our hearts."*[25]

AGAIN, WHY ALL THE BARBARISM AND CRUELTY?

Some time ago I had the pleasure of discussing this and related questions with a U. S. Air Force chaplain. We came to two main conclusions which, as we shall see, throw light on the above problem:

1. We all have some sort of freedom to choose among the paths in life which are made available to us. Our freedom, which incidentally proves that we're real *persons,* allows us *choices of paths* in one way or another almost continuously. But we never have any freedom of choice as to the *consequences* of any path we choose. For these consequences are

the built-in properties of the way which we may freely have chosen. For example, though I choose the way of cheating in examinations I cannot choose the consequences of cheating. They are built into the way known as cheating. Cheating I can choose, but not its consequences of possible discovery or of guilt. Similarly, I may freely choose to abuse drugs—it's entirely my own choice. But, having chosen this way, I cannot *choose* the consequences of drug abuse such as drug dependence, liver necrosis, delirium tremens or hallucinations. They may be built into the path of drug abuse. I may choose alcohol, but I cannot choose whether or not to suffer from the cirrhotic liver which may be a consequence of alcohol abuse. Again, the choice of the way is free, but not its consequences.

I may have the free choice of a mountain or a lowland road. If I freely choose the mountain road, I cannot, after that choice is made, choose or avoid the hill-climbing. Climbing hills and descending into valleys are built into the situation after the choice of the mountain road has been made.

Man chose and still chooses to turn his back on the only good—God. Before doing this he was automatically part of paradise, for paradise was *everywhere* that God was. Having chosen good (God), paradise could not be chosen—it was part of the way with God, paradise was "built in" it. Of course, paradise included eternal life and abundant life. However, later, in turning his back on God, the good one, man refused *the way* of paradise and chose the alternative way built into the choice of following Satan. The built-in consequences included such matters as thistles, thorns, snares, pain, sorrow and death. Thus man found that after making his perfectly free choice for Satan, he automatically began to reap the built-in results of this choice. He found himself "under the harrow"—the "harrow" being part of the way he chose, but which now he could by no means avoid. Of course, the "harrow" is barbarous, cruel and painful in the extreme. But mankind, both in its first father, Adam, and later individually, freely chose this way but now cannot avoid the consequences.

What can be done about the situation? To get man out from "under the harrow," to pull "the tines" out of his flesh, now that they are there, is painful too. Piercing flesh hurts in the first place, but so does pulling out tines. Both running tines through him as he went under the harrow as well as undoing this kind of transfixion can be barbarously cruel. So suffering can originate from either source—the "fall" or the "cure of the fall."

2. Suffering is not necessarily a judgment. Christ has assured us on that point.[26] In a way, "going under the harrow" was a judgment—the judgment following a wrong choice. But "getting out from under the harrow," curing the consequences of the fall, is excruciatingly painful too. When we suffer, then, the pain may be either punitive (putting the tines in), or curative (pulling them out). It may also be a mixture of the two. Until we get behind the scenes of the material life, we shall probably never be able to sort out the two. Nevertheless, both kinds of agony can serve to heal us.

IMPORTANCE OF THE STAKES

There is just one more point to be made in dealing with our problem. Probably few of us really know what we believe until we are asked to suffer some inconvenience or even pain for it. How much are we willing to suffer for what we believe? The *length* we go along that road shows the *depth* of our belief. The Bible holds up Christ as an example—he suffered unto death because he totally believed in redeeming us. Some, like Falstaff, run away to fight another day, believing that discretion is the better part of valor. Surely such persons have shallow faith in what they fight for!

Christ loved his own right up to the cruel death on the cross. This fact establishes forever his absolute faith in his calling to redeem the world. Second, it establishes the degree of his love toward those whom he purposes to redeem.

Therefore, it is obvious that suffering may act as a sieve or filter to sift out the lighter elements of love and faith and separate them from the deeper ones. Suffering may show us what we really do believe as compared to what are only words and hot air. The little suffering that I personally have experienced has certainly shown me the shallowness of my faith in many directions. Suffering produces a clarity of thought in these matters. He who suffers in the flesh has ceased from sin.[27] And clarity in this area of what is sin and what is not sin is vital. For it has led me to repentance at the sight of my own shallowness in eternal matters. Therefore, suffering can act as the filter I personally need to sort out the wheat from the chaff in my own dealings with God, the good one. Fire must separate the dross from the gold in normal refining processes. But after undergoing the fire, the gold is pure gold, though it may be less in volume than before the fiery refining process. Similarly, strong winds blow away the chaff and leave the corn.

THE JOY OF RELIEF

In C. S. Lewis' famous *Screwtape Letters* the "Law of Undulation" is used to describe the ups and downs to which all humans are subject. If we experience heights of joy we shall also experience depths of misery. This is a perfectly normal process to which all flesh is heir.

This idea may be applied to our interpretation of the suffering of mankind. The person who has experienced the horrors of great pain is the most thankful, positively grateful, for any periods in which he experiences less or no pain. How glad the sufferer is when he finds his pains are diminishing. Such joy is unknown to the man who has not experienced pain. Even the pains of "getting out from under the harrow" can lead to this sort of joy which has its actual spring in agony.

The apostle John in the Revelation speaks of this type of exultation when he describes the arrival in heaven of those "who came out of great tribulation."[28] By very contrast, that which they had suffered made their joy the greater. When all tribulation, sorrow, suffering, separation and death are forever behind us, how great will be that joy! But the greater joy will be experienced by those who, in consequence of their faithfulness to him, came out of great tribulation directly to the way of him at whose right hand are joys forevermore.

It may be legitimately asked why the fall of man should have of necessity brought the suffering and death of which the Bible speaks. One can understand it having brought suffering and death to Adam and perhaps to his direct descendants. But why should the consequences of his sin extend to the rest of the world? It does not help much to maintain that Adam was the head of the visible creation which fell and that it fell with him. For the real question is why should this be the case. The creation under Adam was not rational as was Adam and therefore could not possibly bear the guilt that he, being rational but sinful, had to bear.

Our answer to this vital question really depends on our conception of the *state of nature before the fall of Adam.* When the Bible maintains that death and decay did not occur before Adam's fall, it is really introducing a concept which is entirely beyond the power of mortal man today to conceive of. For the idea of no death and decay cuts clean across our total experience of the laws of thermodynamics, particularly the second law. It implies no aging—no entropy increase. The second law states that although the total energy in the cosmos remains constant, the amount of energy available to do useful work in the cosmos is always getting smaller with the passage of time. The sink of energy in the universe which we can no longer use is continually increasing. As I have pointed out elsewhere, this again brings with it the concept that chaos, orderlessness and decay are always on the increase with the passage of time in our total cosmos.[29] Decay and increase in disorder are coupled to increasing time.

Illness, decay, suffering and death can be regarded as accompanying symptoms of entropy increase. In fact, we measure the passage of time itself, in the last analysis, by the rate of entropy increase—how fast a clock, atomic or otherwise, runs down or its entropy increases. Without increase in entropy we would be without time and its measurement. The corollary holds equally well that without time there could be no increase in entropy. The same meaning that is conveyed by "timelessness" and "no entropy increase" could be communicated by saying that an "eternal" or changeless state had been reached.

The creation of Adam, as described in Genesis, corresponds roughly to this eternal state of affairs. For we are introduced to him in Genesis not as a growing baby or as a maturing young man but as an ageless person. Even Eve, produced from Adam's flesh, was apparently ageless too—she was, at least, no infant when she appeared to Adam. In their innocent state there is no record of their having children, although Eve certainly had the sexual organs of a woman and Adam had those of a man. If they lived in a pre-fall world where no decay, no death and no second law of thermodynamics ruled, then reproduction there was not necessary—and, indeed, would probably have been an anachronism.

A consequence of all this is that a species living in a world in which the second law did not obtain must have been vastly different from the present species. Their properties and characteristics must have been very different from what we would expect today where the second law reigns supreme. For example, Adam before the fall could walk and talk freely with the Eternal, whose infinite dimensions he experienced as a matter of course. Traces of this ability are still seen in Moses and some of the prophets who moved in the eternal realm much more easily than we do. Christ did too.

If these considerations concerning Adam's state before his fall are correct, then everything in that primeval state must have been permanent or "eternal"—without time, entropy increase or decay, as they are in heaven or paradise. If the fall took place in such conditions of eternity and these eternal conditions had remained after the fall, this would have meant that the fall and its consequences would have been eternal too, and therefore irreversible. If the eternal conditions existing before the fall had remained unchanged, there would have been no way back from the fall. Adam would have turned his back eternally upon God and good, and his chances of returning would have been ruined forever. His sin would have been an eternal sin, and hopelessness would have remained his lot forever. This is probably the state of the lost angels and Satan who, living in eternity where no change in time can be, are lost forever.

Presumably, then, for this reason God threw Adam and Eve, and the creation over which they had been set, out of eternity and its permanence in paradise, casting them into time with its fleetingness and decay, sorrow and death. God introduced, in fact, the second law, the law of impermanence and death, as a measure to counteract the "freezing" of Adam's fall by making Adam's kingdom and its sin subject to time and its passing. He placed man and all nature in time, with its consequences of sorrow, suffering and death, as a means of keeping man's sin from remaining eternally "frozen" and as a means of providing a way back into the kingdom of love for which he had created man.

Death and decay, having been introduced as a means of providing a way back, became fully developed as this means when Christ used death to overcome the fall on the cross. *This made the second law, and its accompanying culmination in death, the grand highway back from the fall to the kingdom, thus confirming what we have said above about their significance.* Of course, the introduction of death and decay to biology introduced the necessity of reproduction, which did not exist in the realm of the eternal—just as it does not exist in the realms of angels, who are neither married nor given in marriage. Reproduction is a consequence, at least to some extent, of the introduction of suffering, sorrow and death.

ADAM WAS A MAN AND EVE A WOMAN BEFORE THE FALL

The undoing of the consequences of the fall is best seen in Christ's deed on the cross. On dealing with the cause of the fall—rejection of the love of doing God's known will—in embracing God's will, Christ in the flesh with all its sorrows became Christ the *immortal Man,* ("the last Adam," the ideal species of man) rejoicing at the right hand of God. The undoing of the causes of the fall undid the consequences of the fall. Man, first of all in Christ, then took on the properties and attributes of the originally created species known as man. He could again move in time and eternity with equal facility, as demonstrated at his meeting with the disciples on the Emmaus road after his resurrection. The same process (the reopening of paradise) is open to all who wish for it and seek it in the same way that Christ did. The process of the way back begins in man by his seeking Christ's mind on these matters.

The conclusion we draw, then, as far as our original question is concerned, is that time and its concomitant decay, sorrow, suffering and death were introduced to the whole of Adam's cosmos so as to make a way back possible for Adam's cosmos. If Adam and his kingdom had remained in the perfection of eternity, then Adam's sin would have remained forever "frozen." Seen in this light, the tortures of our present time would seem to be necessary mercies consistent with a God intent on restoring to man and his cosmos a kingdom of love, and intent on restoring Adam to his own image.

The undoing of creation was accompanied by the introduction of the second law and its concomitant decay and death. This is really the opposite of creation and its concomitant decrease in entropy. The abolition of the second law, sorrow, suffering and death, is, in reality the same thing as re-creation and is spoken of as such in the Revelation of John.[30]

summary

Our world has come in the last few decades to believe that life and the universe in general are meaningless and absurd. Camus was awarded the Nobel Prize for his persuasive development of this theme. The corollary to this, is, of course, that the accompaniments of life, such as suffering, disease and death, are also meaningless. But, we have not been able to avoid suffering, disease and death, even though they may be absurd and highly distasteful to us all. Not being able to avoid these painful but absurd facts has precipitated a despair in our present generation which surely is unparalleled in recent history. Yet it is the perfectly natural, logical result of the teachings of Camus, Sartre and their predecessors.

If despair has not overtaken all it is simply because some have seen the danger and turned to the hedonism of the hippy and other similar movements: "Eat, drink and be merry, for tomorrow we die." One can understand their conclusion that such an attitude is better than blank despair at the absurdity of it all. To revolt against this situation, to think it can be rectified by revolt leading to better legislation, is to revert to Don Quixotism. And yet, that is what the doctrine of revolt, which is taught in intellectual circles today, is advocating. We are not saying that better laws are not needed. They are. But they will not repair the despair or the fruitless hedonism into which we have fallen. For only new ways of thought and a new *Weltanschauung* can help here.

In this present work the problem of the meaning, if any, of the hodgepodge of good and evil, suffering and pain, justice and injustice, death and life, which we see all around us, is discussed. This problem has led many, particularly intellectuals, into agnosticism and, indeed, into atheism. If God made the good and is omnipotent, who made the bad? If he made both the good and the bad, as the Muslims apparently believe, then he must be the devil. Baudelaire came to this conclusion. But was God really responsible for evil as well as for good?

This book attempts to give some fundamental answers to these questions. It does not profess to go into the details of the case. It only tries to handle the principles, if any, behind the mess in which man and the biological world in general find themselves. As far as I can see, there is no direct answer as to why, for example, innocent people should suffer ghastly accidents on the highways. Nor can we give a primary answer to why six or seven million Jews should have suffered in the concentration camps of Europe. Even less can we account for individual cases of dreadful suffering of which we are all aware. But we can try to give answers to the fundamental questions of evil and good. These answers may help each of us in our own tribulation to apply the principles to individuals, particularly ourselves.

The book points out that the evil we see all around us presents no sound reason for abrogating the good behind the creation. Nevertheless, suffering, illness, war, famine, and pestilence all need interpretation if we are going to bear them sanely. The Lord Jesus tried to instruct his disciples as to the meaning of his approaching suffering of crucifixion and humiliation so that they could bear it better by knowing its meaning. But the disciples were poor students and were overwhelmed by the horror of the event when it burst upon them. This book is an attempt to repeat the instruction in terms of modern problems, using modern terminology. For suffering of one kind or another awaits most of us. If we understand the principles behind it, we shall be better able to bear it when it comes.

Chapter 1 explains why, in a world which gives itself over to the despair of the irrational and the absurd, man needs to reestablish rational thought patterns in order to find intellectually satisfying answers to the paradox of pain.

Chapters 2 and 3 deal with the problem of evil as the atheists and Marxists see it—as a reason for unbelief. The fallacy of this view will become obvious on reading the chapters. Chapter 4 presents illustrations which throw the whole problem of evil and its origin into focus. It also deals with the nature of personality, both divine and human, together with the necessity of free choice if a kingdom of love is ever to be established. It brings out the necessary possibility of evil if one is to have the fact of real good. Chapter 5 shows the way God is treading in order to restore man from the consequences of the fall. It points out that his love is patient and kind, long-suffering and forebearing in his courting humanity back to himself and the ultimate good. Chapter 6 deals with the restoration of man to beauty by pointing out the way in which Christ was exalted. Suffering made even the Son of God mature and perfect. The disciple, not being above his Master, must welcome and undergo the same kind of remedial therapy.

It would be futile to imagine that all questions in this vast problem have been answered in such a short space. They have not. But we trust that a beginning has been made in exposing the principles laid down in the Holy Scriptures for understanding the chaos in which we find ourselves. It is the chaos of a revolution—a revolution of character, having as its end the exaltation and perfection of human beings made in God's image.

appendix

No discussion of the implications of free will would ever be complete without mentioning the problem of predestination or "no free will." There is no doubt about the fact that both propositions, free will and "no free will," are treated in the Holy Scriptures as if they existed side by side without canceling one another out. Thus, the whole subject is a difficult one and ought to be treated by a theologian rather than a mere scientist. However, this book has argued very heavily from the standpoint of free will, so it could be deemed biased, perhaps even tendentious, if we fail to mention that the so-called opposite doctrine of predestination or "no free will" does play an important role too. This was emphasized by Calvin, of course.

Can free will exist side by side with predestination or "no free will" without the two concepts mutually canceling one another out or producing nonsense? The Scriptures teach that they can and do exist side by side without annihilating one another. A comparison of a few texts, as set out in Table I, will serve to confirm the above concept:

TABLE I

Passages Teaching Free Will	Passages Teaching Predestination
"For God so loved the world, that he gave his only begotten son, that *whosoever* believeth in him should not perish, but have eternal life" (John 3:16).	"*You did not choose* me but I chose you . . . I chose you out of the world" (John 15:16,19).

Compare also the following texts conveying a similar sense:

Matt. 11:28	John 11:26	John 12:18	Eph. 1:4
Matt. 8:34	John 12:46	Acts 13:17	James 2:5
Matt. 7:24	Acts 2:21	1 Cor. 1:27	2 Thess. 2:13
Matt. 10:32-33	Acts 10:43		
Matt. 12:50	Rom. 9:33	And many more texts conveying a similar meaning	
Luke 6:47	Rom. 10:11,13		
Luke 12:8	1 John 2:23		
John 4:13	1 John 5:1		

And many texts in the same or similar tenor.

If the passages cited in Table I are compared it will appear that the Scriptures do teach that man is able to say no to God, with all the temporal and eternal consequences of such an action. But the same comparison will also show that man is exhorted to say yes to God and can do so, unless the God who exhorts him is mocking him. But notice something new here. When a man has said yes to God he finds that he was *predestined to do so*. Man was not necessarily predestined to say no, although Judas was *known* prophetically as the son of perdition (foreknowledge). The point is, man is exhorted and wooed to say yes. And he does. But when he accepts the invitation he finds that he was predestined to do so and that God's eternal counsel had foreseen (not *determined*) the affirmative decision. In the case of Judas there was a foreknown no, and in the case of all Christians a predestined yes which emerges when they look back on their free-will decision!

Such a position of free will existing happily side by side with plain predestination obviously cannot be handled by simple logic. From the ordinary human point of view one view excludes the other. A paradox results. Having recognized this paradoxical situation, we must ask, "Is reality (including the reality of free will or 'no free will') intrinsically paradoxical in itself, or is it our *description* of reality which is at fault?"

To decide this point the following must be considered: Reality is multidimensional and probably eternal, whereas we are three dimensional and strictly temporal in our present state. Being temporal, we use means of communication which are temporal and limited in scope. We are thus trying to describe a vast, apparently limitless scheme of reality in terms of a means of communication (language) which is highly restricted, limited, and generally inadequate for the great task demanded of it. To formulate reality, including that of free will and "no free will," in our strictly limited means of description is like trying to describe a probability formula solely in terms of the Arabic digits 1=10 with no alegebra.

To illustrate further, light, as we know it, is a reality, a part of reality, a fact. Our eyes appreciate it without any difficulty at all. However, when we are asked to describe the reality of light by means of communication, we stumble upon untold difficulties. For we can, and do, describe light equally well either as corpuscular or as a wave function. It is, however, perfectly logical to say that if light *is* a wave function then it is certainly not corpuscular in nature. If it is corpuscular, then it is not a wave. The one description excludes the other in terms of normal logic. Nevertheless, modern physics teaches that we must regard light as correctly described only in terms of both wave function and corpuscles. Yet a wave function is not particulate, neither is a particle a pure wave function.

The area of real difficulty is now delineated: Our dilemma with light does not lie in the reality and fact of light itself but in our attempted description of the reality of light in our means of communication. Wave functions and corpuscles as descriptions of one phenomenon certainly do appear to be mutually exclusive from the terminological viewpoint, but they are both united in the reality we call light. Thus the paradox we have noted lies entirely with our description of it in terms of a language and communications medium not built for such complexities. The complexities of light overload our descriptive possibilities, producing apparent paradoxes in the process.

We can try to overcome the apparent contradiction in our description of light by maintaining that light is *either* a wave function *or* a particle simply because it cannot, in our logic, be both at the same time. But if we cut out one description at the expense of the other apparently paradoxical one, saying that light is exclusively a wave function, then we fall into overt error. For this one side of our description is inadequate in describing the reality known as light. *The two antipodes* are necessary to describe the whole of light. The real paradox lies then in our inadequate language rather than in the reality, light.

Returning to free will and "no free will," if we were to maintain that the fact of free will cuts out the possibility of predestination or "no free will" simply because, in our view, the two concepts are mutually exclusive, then we commit the same type of error as we would if we maintained that light, being a wave function, cannot be particulate. To maintain that *either* there is a free will *or* predestination (the two terms being mutually exclusive) is like maintaining that light is *either* a wave function or particulate. If we go on to insist that free will is not capable of existing in the presence of predestination, we are committing the same error we have noted in parallel circumstances in light theory. The fact is that both free will and predestination express multidimensional reality. But we in our strictly restricted view of reality cannot appreciate the fact that the two are congruent and not exclusive. To cut out predestination so as to be able to maintain free will is like cutting out the wave-function description of light so as to be able to maintain corpuscular theory. To effect such a "simplification" is to introduce a false picture of reality. Both concepts are complementary and are a part of reality even though, to our restricted view, they appear to be contradictory.

Thus, we maintain that free will is a reality and so is predestination. It is our limited means of description which makes them appear to be mutually exclusive. Reality contains both, and both describe reality. But we must note one important consequence of this. If frcc will is a reality, in spite of predestination, then all the consequences of free will described in this book operate in full vigor—in spite of predestination which exists alongside it.

Thus, I know that I, of my own free wil, when confronted with Christ, chose not to say no to him. But having said yes to him, I learned afterward that my yes was, in the eternal counsels of God (ultimate reality) a foreknown and predestined yes. "No" is foreknown but, as far as I know, not predestined in the Bible. To eliminate either free will or predestination is to rob reality of one of its aspects which needs to be described by these terms. It is important to realize the difficulties of description in regard to infinity and eternity—phenomena with which our language and thinking apparatus both deal inadequately. But, obviously, for the purposes of this book the one aspect of the truth, that of free will, had to be emphasized to clarify the message. But it would be tendentious to try to eliminate the other side of the coin. If bona-fide free will exists, as the Scriptures and experience maintain it does, then it exists in its full force and with all its consequences as outlined.

It will be obvious from the foregoing that, if God courts man's free-will decisions, he is aiming at influencing him for good. This activity is entirely legitimate and does not interfere with our freedom of action.

The Scriptures teach that there is more in this question than merely influencing our wills for good. There is, working against God's Holy Spirit, also a contrary activity striving to influence man for evil. Just as a personal good one (God) courts our will for good, so a personal evil one (Satan) courts us for ill. The Bible teaches that men do not fight only against flesh and blood in this life but also against spiritual wickedness in "high places." The stark reality of this fact in the struggle for man's will and man's good is underestimated in this day when the masses of people really believe neither in God nor the devil. But a whole book would be necessary to attempt to deal adequately with this struggle.

notes

CHAPTER 1
[1]Julian Huxley, ed., *The Humanist Frame*, p. 42, as cited by Francis
Schaeffer, *The God Who Is There* (London: Hodder & Stoughton, 1968),
pp. 26-27.
[2]See Acts 17:2; 18:4, 19; 24:25.
[3]Cited by Schaeffer, p. 34. Cf. Ps. 30:9-11.

CHAPTER 2
[1]Rom. 1:19-20

CHAPTER 3
[1]Cf. A. E. Wilder Smith, *Man's Origin, Man's Destiny* (Wheaton, Ill.:
Shaw, 1968), and *The Creation of Life* (Wheaton, Ill.: Shaw, 1970).
[2]*Ibid.*
[3]See *Ibid.*
[4]*The Glorious Koran*. Dawood trans. (New York: Daybreak, Penguin
Classics, 1968), p. 23. See also Prov. 16:6.

CHAPTER 4
[1]See Schaeffer, p. 100.
[2]*The Glorious Koran*, pp. 115, 167.
[3]John 3:16, RSV.
[4]Rene A. Spitz, *the Psychoanalytic Study of the Child* (New York:
International Universities, 1945), 1:53; 2:113.
[5]Wilder Smith, *The Creation of Life.*
[6]1 Cor. 1:2l.

CHAPTER 5
[1]Heb. 12:2.
[2]C. S. Lewis, *A Grief Observed* (New York: Seabury, 1961), p. 25.
[3]2 Cor. 4:17.
[4]1 Cor. 13:4-8.
[5]1 Tim. 2:4, RSV.
[6]2 Pet. 3:9.
[7]John 1:9; Rom. 1:19-21.
[8]Prov. 8:31.
[9]John 3:16.
[10]Matt. 6:33.
[11]Heb. 3:7-11, RSV.
[12]Heb. 6:4-6, RSV.
[13]Heb. 10:26-30.

The
Paradox
of
Pain

CHAPTER 6

[1] Lewis, p. 31.
[2] Acts 14:22.
[3] Lewis, p. 25.
[4] *Ibid.*, pp. 25-26.
[5] *Ibid.*
[6] *Ibid.*
[7] Matt. 27:46; cf. Mark 15:34; Ps. 22:1.
[8] Cf. Wilder Smith, *The Drug Users* (Wheaton, Ill.: Shaw, 1969), p. 156.
[9] Heb. 5:7-9, RSV.
[10] 1 Pet. 4:1.
[11] Matt. 10:24.
[12] Phil. 1:29, RSV.
[13] Mark 8:31; 9:12; Matt. 17:12; Luke 9:22; 17:25; 22:15; 24:26, 46; Acts 3:18; 9:16; 17:3; 1 Cor. 12:26; 2 Cor. 1:6; 4:17; Acts 26:23; 2 Tim. 2:12; Matt. 24:9; Col. 1:24; 1 Pet. 5:9; 2 Tim. 1:8; Heb. 11:25, 35; Phil. 3:10; Acts 14:22; Rom. 5:3; 8:35; Gal. 3:4; Phil. 1:29; 2 Thess. 1:5; Heb. 2:18; 5:8; 1 Pet. 2:19, 21; 3:17-18; 4:1, 19. (The sequence is partly in accordance with the word occurrence.)
[14] Phil. 3:7-11, RSV.
[15] 2 Tim. 2:11-12, RSV.
[16] Heb. 2:18, RSV.
[17] 1 Pet. 4:1-2, RSV.
[18] 1 Pet. 2:19, RSV.
[19] 1 Pet. 2:21, RSV.
[20] Luke 24:26, RSV.
[21] Luke 24:26, RSV.
[22] Acts 17:2-3, RSV.
[23] 2 Cor. 4:16-17, RSV.
[24] Wilder Smith, *Man's Origin, Man's Destiny,* pp. 170-74.
[25] Rom. 5:3-5, RSV.
[26] Luke 13:4.
[27] 1 Pet. 4:1.
[28] Rev. 7:14.
[29] Wilder Smith, *Man's Origin, Man's Destiny.*
[30] Rev. 21.

bibliography

Arp, Hans. *Fur Theo can Doesburg*. De Stijl, 1932.

Camus, Albert. *Caligula and Cross Purpose*. Trans. Stuart Gilbert. London: Penguin Books, 1947.

Cruikshank, John. *Albert Camus and the Literature of Revolt*. New York: Oxford U. Galaxy Book, 1960.

The Glorious Koran. Dawood trans. New York: Daybreak, Penguin Classics, 1968.

Huxley, Julian. *The Humanist Frame*. New York: Macmillan, 1962.

Lewis, C. S. *A Grief Observed*. New York: Seabury, 1961.

Sartre, Jean-Paul. *Les Essais*. Paris: Baudelaire Series.

———. *The Condemned of Altona*. New York: Knopf, 1964.

———. *Iron in the Soul*. Trans. Gerhard Hopkins. London: Penguin Books, 1950.

———. *Nausea*. Trans. Lloyd Alexander. London: Hamish Hamilton, 1962.

———. *The Reprieve*. Trans. Eric Sutton. London: Penguin Books, 1945.

Schaeffer, Francis. *The God Who Is There*. London: Hodder & Stoughton, 1968.

Spitz, Rene A. *The Psychoanalytic Study of the Child*. 2 vols. New York: International University, 1945.

Wilder Smith, A. E. *The Creation of Life*. Wheaton, Ill.: Shaw, 1970.

———. *Man's Origin, Man's Destiny*. Wheaton, Ill.: Shaw, 1968.

———. *The Drug Users*. Wheaton, Ill.: Shaw, 1969.